Love-Life of a
Smile

Smile!
Baby!
Smile!

Articulated
Conceived, Composed
Illustrated, Designed and Researched
By
Ramsaran Arora Punjabi

DNA'd in India in 1937

Oriented in schools for 28 years

Self imported to the USA in 1969

Only partially homogenized for 39 years

Cultivated and adulterated by Indians and Americans

AuthorHouse™
1663 Liberty Drive
Bloomington, IN 47403
www.authorhouse.com
Phone: 1-800-839-8640

First published by AuthorHouse 4/15/2009

ISBN: 978-1-4389-6859-9 (sc)

Library of Congress Control Number: 2009903072

Printed in the United States of America
Bloomington, Indiana

This book is printed on acid-free paper.

LOVE-LIFE
OF A SMILE

Life may be awful or
wonderful
It is mesmerizing
nevertheless.

When it explores, fights
injustice and seeks progress
It is worth living.

When it examines itself
critically
It is outstanding

When it smiles
And helps others smile
It is Godly.

Love-Life of a
Smile

DNA crafted human-nature poorly
But it gave the mind basic ability
To be very wicked or very lovely
Why did it then happen naturally!
To be good is hard, to be evil easy
Think for a little while
Wisdom has only one profile
To live a life
By love and smile

Smile Decorated
Fortunate Faces

Love-Life of a SMILE
Dedicated to Frigid Faces

A smile
is
An eternal
Miracle
of
Life

THE IMPRESSION!

I want to impress upon
YOU
An infallible
Impression

If you want to leave
Your best impression
Anywhere any time

Do it
Say it
Work it
With a SMILE

Smile radiates friendship, invites new friends, makes your environment brighter, lightens your mental loads, attracts you to strangers, makes your success easy, renders you conspicuous, strengthens your confidence, begins many new relationships, kills bad feelings, sprouts peace and declares that you are people friendly.

CONTENTS

The sum total of all the contents of this work is only ONE

Simply ONE!

All excretions from our bodies, without any exception, are obnoxious, no matter how and from which part or hole of our bodies they ooze out .They are so smelly, dangerous and repulsive that we want to discard them ASAP. It is puzzling to grasp why a moving biological systems, i.e., animals had to be designed with this kind of nauseating tragedy.

There is one and only one excretion, rather emission that humans can be proud of, and that is an expression on their face of joy and happiness emitted in the form called *SMILE*.

SMILE is the only emission that is longed-for anytime anywhere.

It is easy to remember!

We can think of *SMILE* as the only bodily aroma that does not have to be veiled.

So, keep on smiling, for that is the only, and genetically the best thing you can do with the most exhibited part of your body, your face. Tongue, when you put it to use, remember, is your best friend and also the worst enemy.

A gentle and sweet tongue encased in two smiling lips makes the most powerful impression that one can and should be proud of.

SMILE
OF
DIVINE NERDY ALMIGHTY
(DNA)

I'm the Divine Nerdy Almighty
Hiding mysteries of life molecularly

Your soul and your interior
Your life and your exterior
Your beginning and your expedition
Your love of life and final annihilation
The beginning of you, right from birth
The ageing and the end of you, to death
Are all embedded in a trillionth of an inch
That is I, DIVINE NERDY ALMIGHTY

From Me springs up a mosquito or an ant
Also a giant tree or a huge elephant
In Me is the blueprint, so incomprehensible
So immensely cosmic and so perplexing
I've not bestowed upon you with the
biochemistry
To come close to peer into My mystery

Your conjecture
I'm only a few billion years old
Is ridiculously rude
You shall never comprehend
Why you were born

And why you shall end up dead

Some life I endow with super-
consciousness
Some with micro-mini awareness
I'm extremely tiny and unpretentious
But also gigantic and multifarious
Mostly I bestow perfect and flawless life
Sometimes I fail and cause immense strife

I am the Almighty of Life
From the very beginning of time
God, the supreme creator
Has been my director and maker

I heal your wound
And let you expound
When you blow up your brain
To please your prophet in the heaven

It is your mind,
That is you, your soul and your life
Wherein you hide your mind and soul
Is the puzzle I can't explicate
If you want to feel fortunate
Stride with a smile
All your life all the time

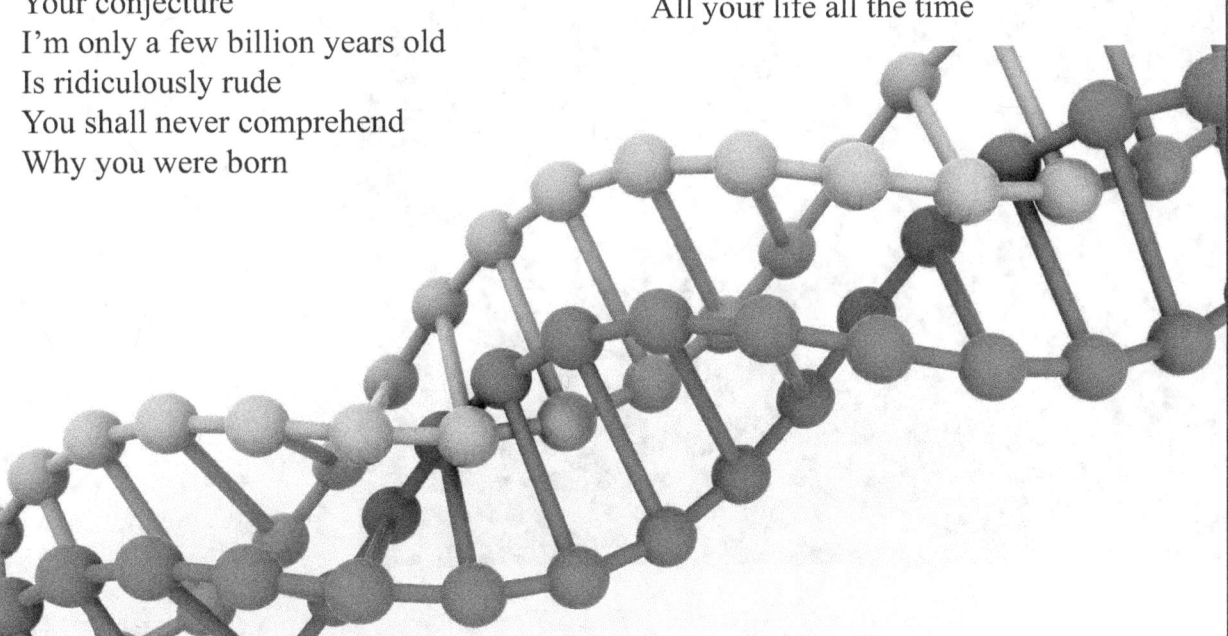

SMILE OF PEACE

The only Religion
The only True Religion
The only lasting Religion
Is the religion of
Non-Violence
By Thought
By Speech
By Action

Believe in It
Practice It
Live by It
Think by It
Walk by It

It will give You
All you need
All you want
All You love

Every violent person is
Menace to himself
And to all
Joy will never see him
Peace will shun him

Smile of non-violence
Is the ultimate
And eternal
SMILE OF PEACE

PATH FOR SUCCESS AND HAPPINESS THE MEANING AND ESSENCE OF LIFE THIS ALL MUST GO WITH A SMILE

In a far-reaching sense, every particle, element, body of any size or description in the universe is linked up with all the rest. This could be called universal link or communication. Any movement of any particle alters position and state of energy of all the rest. There is no such phenomenon as freedom or independence. This is the Supreme Law of the Supreme Power. Also, no such miracle as absolute rest or motion exists.

The links among humans are tiny part of the universal links. However, all humans are linked with each other. All through documented and undocumented history humans in any part of the world have sooner or later altered the destiny of the rest.

Happiness in life is not possible without good communication. In fact, life is all about communication with our parents, children, friends, bosses, subordinates, customers and most importantly government morons. Attentive listening is more important than talking for good communication. Listening is twice as crucial as talking because each one mouth is stationed between two ears. Sending a message, making an announcement, entering into any conversation, asking for a favor, writing a letter, touching and holding someone, are all elements of communication.

Careful observation will show that larger component of communication is gestural. How we position our face, aim our eyes, set our lips, wrinkle our forehead, park our necks, move our arms, point our hands and curve our torsos show and expose our intention, attention, sincerity and respect for those who are talking to us. Arrogance, kindness or humility simply dribbles down one's face and eyes. Ordinary people cannot fake gestures; great actors are great simply because they can wear any expression.

Whether it is the first, middle, last or lasting impression, an attire contributes only a little to it. How, how much and what pours out of the mouth and eyes and how ears receive what is aimed at them determine the impressions that are interchanged at any communication. And a smile is the most important ingredient of all this communication for the best impressions.

WOMAN'S SMILE IS SUPERIOR TO MAN'S

The anatomical and physiological differences between man and woman are well established and indisputable. How the minds of the two differ depends on some biological and many cultural factors and is open to debate. But it is true that man, the macho virility, for thousands of years and until now has been unjust, repressive, and torturous to woman even though her mind is superior to his in many respects.

It appears that due to the evolutionary process the biological function for bearing children makes woman, at least temporarily, physically dependent on man. Woman's routine task of raising children is much more demanding, difficult and crucial than man's traditional responsibility of making a living. For thousands of years, man has been using his freedom from his own offspring to roam the world like a beast. And he used this liberty to invade and massacre his own kind without any feeling of remorse. He has never stopped plundering the planet for fun and excitement. Peace has never been his goal. Whenever his might permitted, he enjoyed enslaving and torturing the weak.

From the limited political power women have had during the last thousand years, and the cultural equality they were accorded in some parts of the world, we could safely conclude that relative to men, women love peace more than wars, they would not go on massacre binges, they would believe in and practice liberty and equality more sincerely, and they would rule more humanly and organize more efficiently, and they would promote friendship and harmony to the best of their ability.

Now scientists are discovering that man is truly the weaker sex. He is more impulsive, more dependent, and more susceptible to lack of care. He is a slower learner and has a higher rate of attention deficit disorder. The only reason man climbs up the ladder of success faster is the environment of his own sex. In every country today where woman is being given equal opportunity, she is proving herself superior to man in all aspects of schooling, athletics, debating, organizing, and social activities. She is closer to her family, more caring of her family, more affectionate, and more sacrificing.

Research also shows that baby girls start uttering intelligible words, putting words together, and imitating full sentences faster than baby boys. The emotional brain of boys is primitive relative to that of girls; for that reason, male emotions translate into action with much less deliberation. Due to some anatomical differences, male brains are less versatile in processing information than female brains. Man in most of the world is still engaged in heinous crimes against woman. The most amusing fact is that man has made all his Gods and prophets descend to earth in his own macho form. In many countries he justifies his monstrous acts in the name of his own manly God. Women of the world must unite against the heinous activities of man to free themselves from their chains and add love and smiles to the masses of the world.

A BRIEF STORY OF SMILE

The journey of life begins with a short shrill cry and soon thereafter it blooms into flowery smiles. Every new little life is pure, uncontaminated and genuinely joyful.

Ordinarily life begins accidently without much planning. Planned or not, parents dedicate themselves to make the new life secure, healthy and comfortable. They dream, plan, teach and educate their young to build fortunes and prosper. Schools teach the art of making a living and parents reinforce it. Life starts embodying itself in its mother's womb in one of nature's most mysterious and exceedingly swift processes. The complexity and enormity of this embodiment is baffling. The fetus that starts housing this life grows in a geometric progression. The moment the fetus can start its life independently, it is expelled from its mother's body. Every seed of life holds a never ending infinite succession of seeds of life. Life after birth or rebirth is truly a concept called reincarnation. The material and immaterial components of seed of life are the mysteries that we shall continue to explore forever. Parental upbringing, cultural environment, religious dictates, political corruption and genetic programming shape and scatter young minds for good and evil. The journey of life often ends after prolonged pain and suffering; sometimes it ends tragically. Mostly the end is awaited even by those who loved the journey maker intensely.

The sensation of love wrapped in

LIFE-SIZE SMILES

is the best wreath two lovely arms can offer to the one you love genuinely

LET THE FORTUNE SMILE

Building fortunes continues to be a lifelong dream but few succeed in realizing it. Most fail and give up. Few comprehend that big fortunes are more due to strike of luck than simply a fruit of hard work and dedication. Most end up running their lives from day to day and deal with every hour as it shows up. Pursuit of happiness begins right after basic needs are satisfied. Alas, happiness is not a target that can be arrived at; it is only a path that fortunate few follow.

Life begins to fade and wither away soon after it creates a new life. The mortality of the embodiment of life is immortal. The real life with all its mystery hides in microscopic seeds.

The body is mortal. The life it embodies is immortal. Body starts withering away almost as soon as it is capable of embodying new lives, whether or not it does so.

Ponder the brevity! Life cannot flow freely in a thorny mind. Anger, violence, jealousy, hatred and greed poison life's path. Let the path be simple, lovely, flowery and sunny for one to walk through it with genuine smile. Let the journey end with a smile and not with a fried frown.

Let life smile at whatever it encounters, for this is the true wisdom. Forget not that life is short and its story is too. It fades fast. Simply smile and laugh by yourself and with all around you to continue this journey. Plan to build a fortune but do not forget that a smiling mind and heart is more fortunate than anyone who has built a fortune.

Smile in a way is like an almighty of some special kind. It has power to treat and cure depression, one of the most terrible states of mind and curse to physical health. A smile can cause a chain reaction; just a hearty laughter can alter a dead environment into a vibrant atmosphere. Sunshine brightens the outdoors, but smile cheers up interiors of hearts and minds. We have among us millions of pill popping people (ppp) who have to run their daily life on these pills; the main reason, these ppp have to do what they have to do is that they have few or no smiles around them. They find their life without smile; pills fill the space that smiles leave vacant.

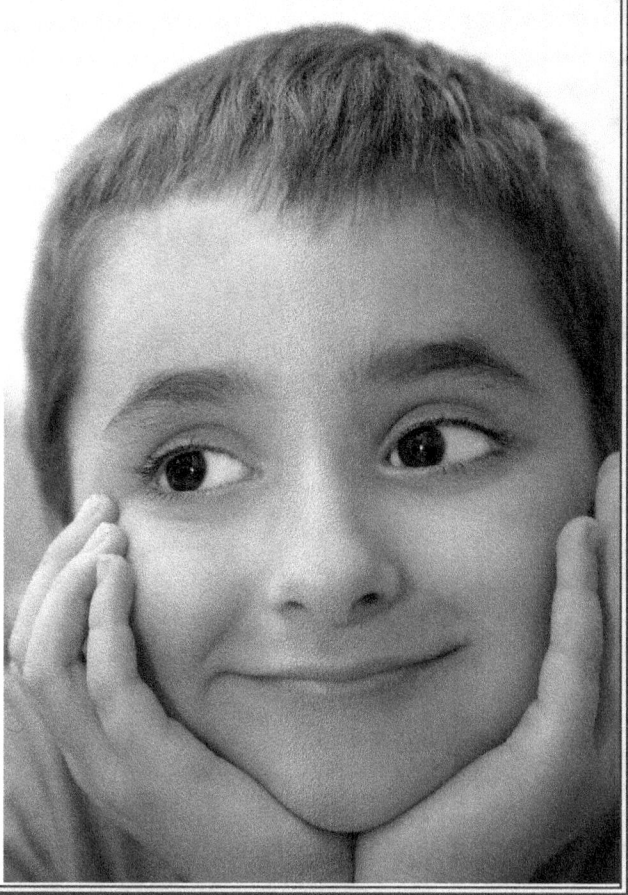

THE ORAL LAW
OF ORATION

To impress audience confidently
To go on with the life peacefully
Unless you want to dupe politically
Don't articulate flamboyantly

To sound brilliant and radiant
Diligent, relevant and intelligent
Let your gestures be modest

You may be an expert evidently
It is persuasive if narrated gently
Whatever you want to convey plausibly

It is true and honest
The law is omnipotent
Evident and persistent
That to **SPEAK SOFTLY**
Sweetly and smilingly
Is divine and saintly

The health and functions of the brain and the heart are intimately interlinked. They communicate with each other neurologically, electromagnetically and emotionally. The blood pressure and blood flow to each other is also closely related. Whatever is heard by the ears, seen by the eyes, tasted and uttered by the tongue, felt by the skin and the internal organs, and smelled by the nose is processed by the brain. Immediately thereafter the brain commands the heart to change it rhythms, blood supply and blood pressure to meet the needs of the mind and rest of the organs. Minor, major and fatal heart attacks can sometimes strike simply from what our senses go through. How we take the external world determines what kind of heart condition we have. It has been multifariously documented that the heart keeps on smiling if it is ruled by a pair of smiling lips.

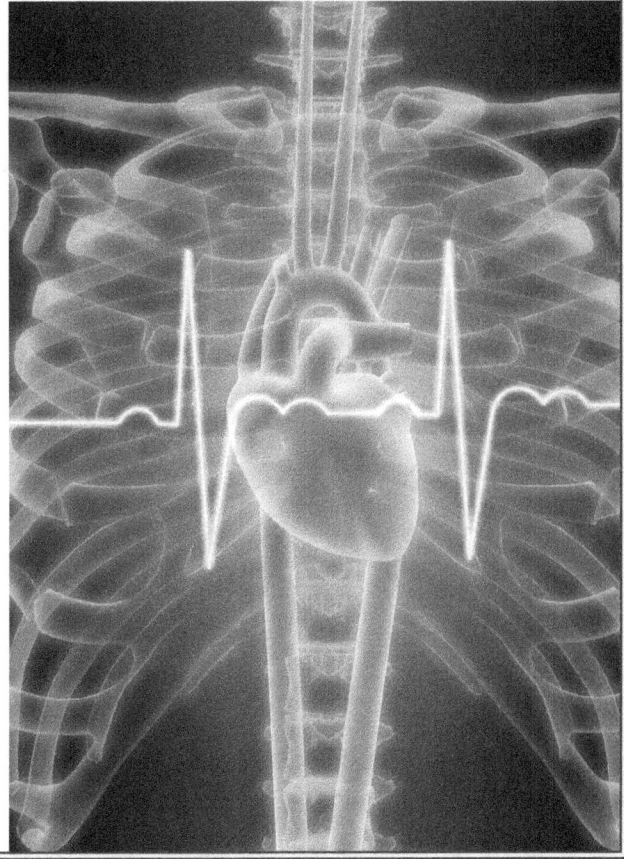

Smile needs no definition, an explanation or a reason for being there, here or wherever. Why, where and how it happens, are interesting questions. For evolutionists, it has to relate to survival. For spiritualists it is associated with peace. For psychologists, it bonds with joy and happiness. For ordinary people it is simply the best gesture one can wear. If you are looking for a mathematical model of smile, you will be disappointed. We can't yet describe life and its activities through mathematical equations. We can witness smile in every culture, at every age, in every nook and corner of the globe. It is imaginable that gesture of smile may not have been omnipresent. A tortured slave, a starved man, a sick child or a shelter-less person can't squirt a smile. Smile has only short existence at a time; a long smile appears funny and thoughtless. Smile may not have much to do with survival of the living, because all life exists for a very limited time.

If we are healthy and have most of the things of life that the majority around us have, any addition to our wealth will make us happier only temporarily. Lottery winners return to their original state of mind very soon after the joy runs its course. Tragedies, too, have a limited unhappy life.

The very mode of thinking that brings us good things of life does not really add to our satisfaction, because this mode becomes an integral part of our way of living and all new gains become new frames of reference for new desires. The theory of relativity is as true for our short lives as it is for the infinite universe for infinite time.

In a nutshell, any pursuit of happy smile is a sign of being unhappy. The happy ones are not aware of being happy. The unhappy ones do not care to use the free recipe that is always at their doorsteps

Optimism has been proven to be an important element of a happy mind. It propels us into positive active emotions, hopefulness, teamwork, and generally toward feelings of love and cooperation. It is also a psychological drug to treat depression. An optimistic mind is normally a busy mind residing in a busy body - creating, inventing, discovering - and so has little time to be unhappy.

It is not poverty that has much to do with crime. Relative difference, visibility, and media exposure between the haves and have-nots are the fires that char the heart of the have-nots who feel justified in attacking others for equality and presumably happiness.

YES
GOD REALLY SMILED
AT ME!

Nothing is wrong with you if you talk to God, because all God fearing people do that regularly. However, if you claim, God talked to you, you would be considered schizophrenic and will be advised to seek psychiatric help.

When I was around sixteen, I believed myself to be a devout Hindu. I had read most of the well-known Hindu epics and religious books. Never missed going to temple on Tuesdays and prayed without demanding and expecting any material goods from God.

Hindu Holy Scriptures claim that it is possible to see or meet God if one is truly devoted to Her and has never done any wrong of any kind to anyone. I had become so deeply and blindly engrossed in worshipping Her without knowing what all the rituals I was engaged in actually meant. I regularly prayed before I went to bed, and I truly believed that I can see God and may even hear Her talking. Experts on the working of mind now know that an imagination can some times take hold of mind so strongly that it can become naturally true.

One morning when I woke up I realized that God Herself came to me in my dream that night. I vividly remember what God looked like. She was a dazzling round light of rainbow colors kind of smiling and spinning, extremely bright but not enough to blind me. The Light also had thousands of designs that looked like eyes. I was awe stricken not knowing what it was. My imagination went wild and I simply uttered "Oh God". I got a response "Yes, I am. Why do you want to see Me?" perhaps in my dream-like imagination.

"Tell me what one should live for." I asked. "First, remember, I do not need a mouth to speak with and you do not need ears to hear Me. You can hear Me directly through your mind. Second, note that for good of all life, for I am Life Itself, if you hurt anyone, you hurt ME. Non-violence is the simplest law that I want you to follow. It means, you do not hurt anyone by your thoughts, words and acts. All life is sacred. Violence is the root cause of all the problems man is facing. I created 'man' for doing good to other creations of Mine, but I am disappointed in him. " God smiled and responded.

"Is that all that is important?" Sitting on my knees, folding my hands in prayer, looking at the dazzles of lights, I inquired again.

"You are on this earth for a long time to enjoy My creations of flowers, foods, sun, sky, ocean, days and nights and loving companionship of other living beings. If you do not burden yourself with greed and never think that you are superior to anyone else, you will be at peace with yourself and Me." God replied.

I always imagined that if I ever met God, I would ask a million questions. Now, when God was right there I had no more questions, because She being there was infinitely more happiness than one could ever ask for.

After that night I was a different person. I told of my dream to none. I thought I was a very special living being. But as time passed by and the parental and societal pressure for being able to earn a livelihood mounted, I forgot my dream. I became just like all the billions of people on our planet. The most important command "For good of all life, for I am Life Itself, if you hurt anyone, you hurt ME" that God gave me in my dream, disappeared from my mind. For me no loss exceeded that loss. My own life has been violent in thoughts, word and actions.

Hindu philosophy of life from very ancient times originated two very important laws, first the law of peace and second the law of Karma. "Om Shanti, Shanti, Shanti" – 'Shanti' is the Sanskrit word for 'peace' - is pronouncement made at the beginning and conclusion of every Hindu religious ceremony and prayer. In simplest term the law of Karma has two meanings. First, do your duty, but do not count on the result you expect, because numerous variables affect the outcome. Second, the outcome of most of your actions in your present life shall stand before you and mock at or make or destroy you.

GOD'S SMILE

One day!
God was strolling around Her galaxies. Her Supreme Angel approached Her. She humbly bowed and begged to ask, "Oh The Almighty!
You have created intelligent life on zillions of planets in Your infinite universe. I have to my dismay noticed this intelligent life called 'man' on planet earth is mutilating the beautiful habitat You created for it. The messengers and prophets You sent to the planet earth have divided men to destroy and hate each other. Why did You have to make 'man' at all?"

"My Angel!" God smiled and responded, "Man is My most fascinating creation. It is an amusement to Me. It falsely fancies that I send My messengers or prophets to its habitat - earth –or any other planet in any form. These self-proclaimed messengers are simply ordinary men; they have done little good but more harm to their confused followers. Man must remember that earth is only like a tiny particle of dust in My infinite universe. The intelligence that I have bestowed upon any life is so infinitely minuscule that it can never comprehend My mysteries, immensity, minuteness and Me. Look at the fun I see in man's activities. It has built huge structures to house Me, gigantic statues to represent Me, and large enclosures for My safety; sacrificed animals and its own young to please Me; created songs and music to entertain Me; clothed and decorated Me with glittering costumes and the most beautiful flowers to make Me look more attractive; painted Me with rainbow colors in wild imagination; elevated some of its own kind to see and meet Me; fed Me gourmet foods; invented religions to approach, and find Me; prayed to Me for more earthly possessions; begged of Me to bring the dead to life. Look, man is as much a funny creation to Me as I am to man's imagination. Man is the best toy I could create We Both would be bored without Each Other I do not, therefore, intend to change man's life style any time soon."

SMILE OF THE MIND

Mind - the master that runs the incredible human machine - expands, shrinks, matures for better or worse, in many more vivid ways than the body it occupies. It is no less puzzling than the mystifying universe. We are at any time all and only that our minds hold.

The mind takes birth with a blank slate. Engrossed in its body, it writes unto itself during the early years of its life countless prejudices, false notions, and erroneous judgments. It is possible but exceedingly difficult to correct all that is deeply engraved in its gigantic capacity.

The structure of elements of genetics is little known out of its immensity of complexity. The mind shall continue to be the real perplexity. Let the mind comprehend itself to change the course of its activity for a tranquil life full of smiles

Smile plays an important role in running every life. Every moment of every day from the very beginning to the very end of every day, smile has a space it must occupy; perform its chores and go to sleep only when its carrier dozes off. Its absence can execute havocs, and presence carries out strange and difficult operations of both happy and unhappy living. How to realize and apply its latent attributes should be taught as a prerequisite for earning any academic degree of value. Humor, laughter and soft speech are all other vital elements of any life worth living.

Smile is the component of non-verbal communication that is more effective than all other gestures, namely, bodily posture, eye movement and forehead wrinkles and crinkles. Smile beautifies and decorates a face more attractively than all necklaces, ear rings, diamonds, beauty aids and hair styles combined. Smile is not cheap, shoddy, stingy or mean; it is precious but free, impacting but soft, enriching but emancipating.

SMILE AND HAPPINESS

A smile is an articulation of a happy disposition. A happy disposition is a smile's verbalization. Happiness propagates seeds of a smile Smile propagates seeds of a happy life With a smile you are closer to confidence Confidence puts you on the path of success

Smile shall turn you into an optimistic person. You shall always see the glass half full not half empty. A positive outlook into future is important to see positive outcome. Mood determines the mode of thinking. And mode of thinking determines whether one floats or sinks.

A genuine smile is the most important element of any gesture of goodwill. It communicates kindness, love, friendship, care, support, generosity, helpfulness and all that is good in the smile-giver's temperament. A smile is rarely returned with a frown, anger or aggression. A smile initiates all peace-processes.

Smile is the most pleasant element of body language. Body language is as important as spoken words in verbal communication. Eyes play a vital role in this process. A sincere smile is always accompanied by a special radiance from the eyes.

Smile

If your are empty
And want to be happy

You are shy
And can't fly

Or you are lonely
And want to be friendly

To feel like a power
Or bloom like a flower

To spin in victory
Or search out the eternity

To pay for all your sins
Or to fight your fears

If you are no one
Or want to be someone

To welcome your
sweetheart
Or leave your imprint

Simply Smile!

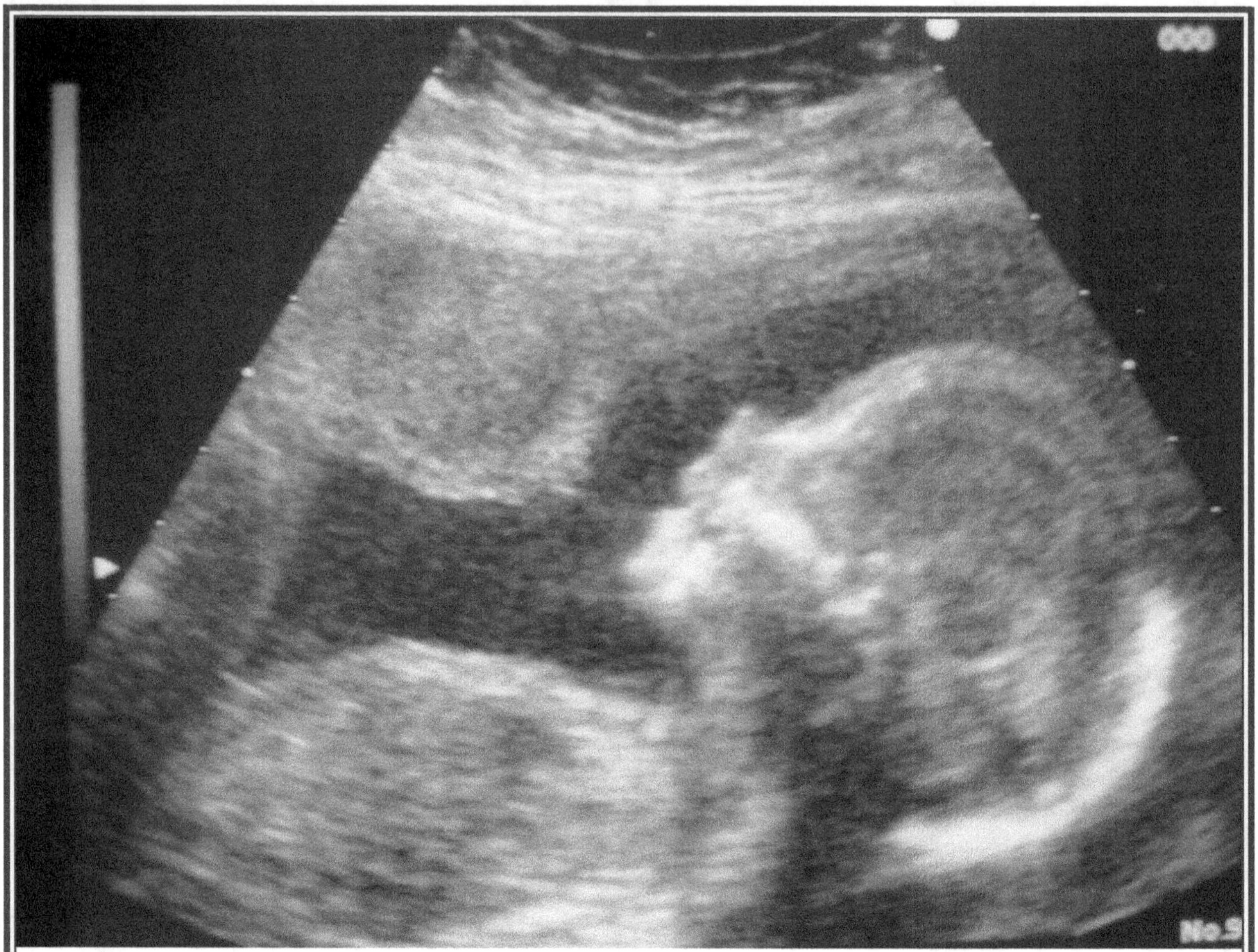

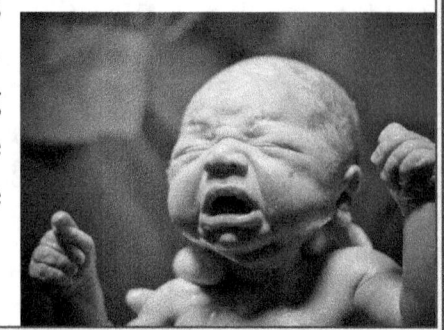

Smile is built into DNA or its gene-components. All changes and activities in a living body are programmed into its DNA. Meticulous observations have confirmed fetus smiling. Few weeks old infants smile to varying degrees; they smile when they are awake and sometimes when asleep. Spontaneous smile were observed even when they are kind of half asleep, without and with any external funny environment. Why infants smile, is more or less a mystery.

It is also a mystery why only a human- offspring cries at the very moment it exits its birth canal. The argument that a cry initiates breathing does not appear to be true because none of the mammals closest to humans make any noise for a pretty long time after birth.

SMILE OF MISFORTUNES

December 2005, I was flying from Detroit to New Delhi via London. At London an Indian about 55 years old boarded the plane and occupied the seat next to me. I welcomed him and asked him if he was visiting England from India or he lived in England. He liked my talking to him because he smiled and appeared very friendly. He told me he came to UK some 35 years ago following a friend who also came there from the same village and was making very good living.

This man was a Sikh and was born in the Indian state of Punjab. Sikhs generally are very true and honest to their religion; they are very hard working and helpful to each other. They are sincerely respectful in their business and personal dealings. Their prophet Gurunanakdev taught only love, respect, tolerance and a disciplined living. They should be rated as one of the best set of people in the world.

We had many hours of flight from London to New Delhi. He told me his name was Sukhdev Singh, and had a very prosperous manufacturing business in a suburb of London. He had 135 employees, and did not know what to do with his money. Every year his one-month vacation consisted of only visiting his birth-village in Punjab and to chat, eat, walk and sit with his childhood friends. There was no joy more important than that he could think of.

When I asked him if he had any family and kids in UK, I could see his eyes watering and his face very sad. I kept quiet and did not repeat my question. He, however, after a deep silence, started telling me his life history. He came to UK with nothing in his hand; he had no education. After borrowing a little money from his friend he bought a lathe for some repair work. His customers were so happy with him that they brought a lot of referrals. Within five years he had a machine shop employing 50 workers. In the meantime he returned to his village; his father had already arranged a bride for him. He was happily married to a typical family devoted very sweet Punjabi girl. With her he returned to his business in UK. Within a four years span he was blessed with two handsome sons. The boys started growing up with all the good things and toys of life at their feet sooner than they asked for. His sons were envy of their friends among all relatives, and kids at school. They had best of clothes and shoes. They were the only ones being chauffeured to school in the latest model cars. They were being fed the richest and high fat foods. Their mother was illiterate like their father. She did not think much of education. With all the money she believed his sons will take over their father's prosperous business and will be set in their lives. The boys grew fast. Drinking is a common feature of all Sikh men. The boys took to drinking too at an early age. Sukhdev told me all the above in a very depresses mood. Finally he concluded. One of his two sons had fatal heart attack at twenty-one, for he was severely over weight and had not engage in any physical activity. His other son while drunk ran his motorbike into a tree and died instantaneously.

A very sad true story it was. When approaching New Delhi, air hostess gave us both disembarking forms. Sukhdev asked me to fill up his form, which I did. I told him I should not sign for him. When he signed his form, I could see he could only scribble his name. He could hardly write any other words. I had borrowed his pen to complete the forms. He asked me to keep the pen; it was a very expensive pen with the name of his company inscribed on it.

When our plane was landing Sukhdev said he truly believed that it is all the fruit of actions in our past lives. This was all that God ordained for him and he was peaceful and content with what he had left. When he would reach his village and meet his childhood friends, he would only remember the joys, laughter and smiles of his very early years and pains of his adult life would disappear.

Can man discover any convincing evidence that he is not a robot – a bio-robot! Is it only a matter of incalculable degree of complexity that sets apart - man and a bio-robot.

Man's all physiological and anatomical systems have only one purpose, that is, to keep the brain ticking. No matter what, if the mind – the material brain – stops ticking, all rest of the bodily systems are useless, worthless, and meaningless. Very puzzling is the puzzle, why God had to be infinitely insane to design and build an infinitely complex system to house a few pounds of neurons. This ticking mass of neurons is strangely claimed to give shelter to life, love, loveliness loneliness, etc., etc. And the seat of mysterious 'consciousness' appears to be more uncertain as 'consciousness' itself goes around looking for its location.

The man - that God designed - is simply a mysterious mass that is made to react to sights, smells, sounds, scenes and signs to yield sorrow, sadness and smile. A glorious word 'emotion' was invented by the man to glorify his existence.

Was reproduction -perpetuation of species – in God's mind. God cannot be worried about such trivial stuff, for She has zillions of plans to execute in Her endless kingdom.

What a chaos! God created man without any fanfare and celebration; She didn't think much of Her man. In return God's man created many Gods, over and over again; he also created God's sons, moms, and countless representatives.

A man bought a parrot to teach it imitating human speech. The parrot flawlessly imitated every word the man spoke. Finally, the man prompted the parrot to repeat "I can fly". The parrot responded, "You are lying".

Oh Man! Your ignorance is boundless. So, just enjoy your short stay on your planet, be happy and keep on smiling.

Exhaustive research and findings by medical doctors, psychologists and biologists have confirmed a very close-knit relationship between physical and mental health. Gesticulation and mental activity are interdependent. A smile is supportive of good mind-body well being.

THE MARVELS OF LIFE:

A smile holding a smile
A smile loving a smile
A smile enjoying a smile
A smile kissing a smile
A smile listening to a smile
A smile beholding a smile
A smile sweetening a smile

FALLING IN LOVE

The beauty of the exterior - skin, eyes, lips, hair, body forms - of the youth and of the infatuations, attacks any eye and heart instantaneously and then the supremacy of the power of procreation assaults all minds to fall into the infallible trap irrespective of the power of the intellect of small and great humans. Many fake smiles go into action in these short encounters of the power of beauty enhanced by the power of a smile.

The slogan *"falling in love"* is the truest measure of the short, fleeting and cunning relationship of the materially rich, technically progressed cultures and societies. They really *fall* many times for short durations and successfully wreck the lives of their innocent children repeatedly.

The cultures that deeply prize love-relationship, love is alive even after death and *"rising in love"* is the slogan that rules.

Let love be ruled by a real smile from the very beginning to the very end of the life to leave the world in some tranquility.

We must strive to keep our noses above all the muck we are imbedded in, for smelling only the roses is the hardest part of living. However, we must find a way to do that. We see only a partial picture of what goes on within and without us because we suffer from biased thinking, very limited knowledge and defective analytic ability. All our conclusions, except those related to scientific observations, are tainted with a variety of spices that we taste all through our lives. Many times, even with our best intentions and plans, we end up committing terrible deeds.

History is mostly the true story of man's horrible nature. It teaches that it cannot teach, for it keeps on repeating itself. It is important to realize that in order to breathe fresh air and to enjoy free sunshine and to let our hearts smile in harmony and tranquility, we have to shake many kinds of nests built into our minds and replace them with right ones

UNREAL REALTY

The number of people popping pills to put their minds at peace is no puny piece of the world population. The pharmaceutical establishment, pharmacies, physicians, and psychologists drive a good amount of their livelihood from restless souls. Progressive technology has invented more gadgets to complicate our lives than to simplify it. People devise intricate life styles to dump themselves into melancholy, loneliness, and despair. The worst culprit is the never-ending thirst for more and more things. Things need physical and mental space and continual maintenance and expense to exist, and they do replace the space that could have been occupied by imaginary happiness at no cost.

Happiness can only be measured on a relative scale. If we are less miserable than those around us, we are less unhappy. Success is an ingredient for being happy, and if others fail and we do not, we are happy. A person with one eye is happier than one without both the eyes. We are happy when we get a raise, but unhappy if our associates get a bigger raise. The less affluent, no matter what their possessions, are unhappy because they keep on comparing themselves with the more affluent. How hard it is, therefore, for them to comprehend the meaning of a smile!

In our daily life we take many very simple steps to convert a desirable smiling life into a rigorous complexity. We take simple, clean, and mostly harmless fruits and produce of nature and apply all our skills, tools, and ingenuity to blend, crush, fry, and destroy most of the natural goodness to invent delicatessens. All entertainment, joy, and fun have been made impossible without a lot of micro-planning, scheduling, traveling, noise, and intricate gadgets.

The constitution, configuration and composition of the universe or its minutest components are so infinitely mysterious that for us to be sure about the real realty in any form or shape is simply an arrogant ignorance and shall remain so forever. Simply speaking, we cannot and shall never know anything for sure. All perception through our physical senses and then translated by our baffling consciousness cannot and should not prove or disprove any concepts, theories or visions. Few laws of nature that we claim to know for sure may change on the time-clock of the universe. On the front of genetics of life, little can be pieced together to comprehend the magic that converts a tiny seed into a gigantic tree or an ovum into an exotic walking talking thinking body. Almost all humanity from times immemorial took birth, lived and perished in pursuit of some illusory happiness, happiness that has never been embodied. If we can grasp clarity of life, nothing should disturb us, nothing should sadden us, and nothing should make us too happy or unhappy. And nothing should prevent us from wearing a smile for that is the only true life-style.

'YOU'
The Mysterious Smile

Don't condemn yourself if you refuse to believe that 'YOU' in you is as elusive as God. You are one of billions who would refuse to think that 'YOU' and God are equally mysterious. The question "What in your body is really YOU?" is very difficult to comprehend; for most this question is ridiculous.

Who or what in your body and bodily systems sees, hears, tastes, feels, talks, screams, smiles, shoots, eats, remembers, plans, takes birth, lives, and finally dies, appears to be an absurd question, because the answer appears to be very obvious. It is 'YOU'. So, when "YOU' are born, what is really born! An indefinable 'YOU' in a cluster of biological cells? And when 'YOU' die, who or what actually dies! Is it an unassailable and unanswerable question!

You will have hard time disagreeing that 'YOU' exists somewhere inside your skull and nowhere else. Where in the skull? The location is impossible to figure out. A simple event, that prevents feeding the interiors of your skull with oxygen for a few minutes, ends the existence of 'YOU'. 'YOU' is gone forever; 'YOU' then shall not come back no matter what is done. The life, existence, concept and activity of 'YOU' is totally, wholly and permanently dependent on unbroken supply of oxygen. The process to keep 'YOU' alive is potently simple. And to kill 'YOU' is also potently simple.
Sophistication is what scholars survive at; they have replaced the real 'YOU' with the concept called 'consciousness'. None of all the scholars since the very dawn of all knowledge and intelligence could figure out whereabouts, form and shape of 'consciousness'. Lack of oxygen for a few minutes is as fatal to it as it is to 'YOU'. So 'YOU' lives inside your skull. This is universally agreed. Now in what shape or form? Anyone, who attempts to answer this question, or claims to know the answer, is either a God or a lunatic. 'YOU' cannot be defined, felt or seen; so how can it be located?

Remember, 'YOU' came into existence instantly, mysteriously and microscopically either inside your mother's womb or in a Petri dish. Infinite quantity of 'YOUs' can be created and annihilated extremely fast. From the inside 'YOU' in blood and flesh are perfectly identical to every member of your specie, from the outside you are only imperfectly identical for your hungers and thirsts are hardly different form the rest of your kind. It is a little bit essential to be sure of your big littleness, little bigness, and immense vulnerability. God is at full liberty to ask you come back without any warning. Alexander, Newton, Pope, Einstein, Lincoln, Gandhi, Buddha, Christ, all were called back without any notice.

The most important characteristic of 'YOU' is that it is the only entity that can move faster than the speed of light. It takes eight minutes for light to reach from sun to earth, but your imagination can take you from earth to sun in an instant. 'YOU' thinks it can think. What thinking really means has been thought of for centuries and no consensus has been reached. The debate among the celebrated thinkers has been about reality. Since they could not comprehend the meaning of reality, any progress in this matter has been impossible. Finally, the truth is that 'YOU' is very small, very vulnerable, very fleeting and very indefinite. This 'YOU' will be very comfortable if it accepts these facts and acts humbly, joyfully and respectfully.

So keep on smiling, for your ignorance is universal; it is pleasant; and it is perpetual. You will never know who you are, where you came from, whereto you are headed, and where you shall end up at the end. Some may believe they shall reach heaven, and some hell, but take for granted whatever may happen, it shall happen only after 'YOU' is converted into the precious and universal dirt 'YOU' was made of to begin with.

THE BUSINESS OF LIFE

Remember!

This fact of life.

Life is a business. The most important business is the business of life. All businesses target on life's business.

So, concentrate on life. This is all that has to be done. It is the simplest task, but for most it the hardest task. The reason why human brain complicates life is because the brain itself is the most complicated creation of the Creator.

How to keep business of life simple?

If you are stupid, you can't keep it simple.

If you are not stupid, you will try your best to make it complicated.

You may try your best to simplify whatever; but the world around you shall try its best that you fail at every step.

And you shall fail at every step.

Simplest meaning of LIFE is:

L =Love

I= Is

F= Fruitful

E=Emotion

Hardest meaning of LIFE is:

L= Lonesomeness

I=Is

F= Fearsome

E=Emptiness

Facial actions, expressions, gestures and articulations with or without any words pouring out of lips make a world of difference on spectators and listeners. Love and hatred, pleasure and pain, joy and sorrow, success and failure, all alter both internal functions and external appearance of any combination of flesh, nerves and blood. The destructive and constructive power of external appearances is immense. Genes crafted shape of forehead, nose, ears, eyes, and skull very soon shows less effect than cultured emotional facial forms. The true business of life is selling; in sophisticated words they call it marketing. We are selling or marketing ourselves for some kind of return every breath of our lives.

Aspiring for love, friendship and joy is hardly different from seeking money, good job or an academic degree. The state of the stuff surrounded by the skull is same in either case. Some goals need one step marketing and some many. You have to market yourself. You have to do it if you are not a kind of Einstein; chances are you are not one. No matter what you have conceived and created, it has to see the light of a market.

Your marketing tools are: Your face, expression on your face, words pouring out of your lips, your bodily decorations. Each one these elements carry their own indispensable weights. Bends, curls and twists on a face make the most important element of marketing one's ideas. A mass of information and knowledge delivered with super intelligence comes next. The curls on a face that exhibit invitation, joy, confidence and sincerity very obviously is truly "a smile".

A MILLION DOLLAR SMILE

Jo was single only 22 and never wanted to marry for he thought he would never have enough money to give a decent life to his kids. He worked like a robot at an assembly plant of GM. He did not have to use his brains to do anything. He started believing that he did not have much of a brain and whatever was there would soon deplete to nothing because it was idle all the time. His routine: for breakfast a two-liter coke bottle and one pound bag of potato chips; lunch consisted of three hot-dogs or two big hamburgers; couple of beers and variety of fast foods, pizza, etc., would suffice for dinner. His 230-pound plus body was least of his worries. He had lifelong medical insurance through his union contract.

He thought himself to be very lucky for he had skill of no value and was still making over $42 an hour simply because he had a union job at an auto maker. In the morning he raced his old Chevy to work and then crawled to this moving assembly line and got busy tightening nuts and bolts around car-bodies. He would anxiously wait for the quitting time to end boredom of everyday and then race back to his same old Chevy he hated to look at. He wondered why he could not drive a brand new Cadillac, like all the GM executives did.

Jo was a great believer in luck. When the great Michigan Lottery started, he would religiously buy five one-dollar tickets every day. It was less than $150 monthly investment out of his $3,000 a month take home pay. Three years went by, and his luck still awaited him. One fine afternoon when he looked at the winning numbers, he looked at one number again and again to make sure that he was not mistaken. He called one of his buddies and asked him to confirm what his eyes were seeing. Sure, his buddy punched at him and screamed "YOU MILLIONAIRE". Jo jumped and screamed, "I quit, and I never have to see this place again." He drove to the nearest bar and drank until he lost himself completely. After a couple of hours he erratically drove to his home. He saw a cop behind his Chevy with red and blue light whirling ordering Jo to pull over. Jo stopped right in the middle of the road and was arrested for drunk driving. He spent that night in the local jail. Next morning at court appearance he had to pay a fine of $500 and warned that at next drunk driving conviction his driving privileges will be suspended.

Now the dreams started being realized. Jo drove to the local Cadillac dealer and ordered the latest model fully loaded convertible Cadillac. Then he ordered a unique feature that the body had to be "GOLD PLATED". The sales person was ecstatic, and said he would have to check on the extra cost. Jo wrote a $100,000 check, and instructed "Don't bother to ask, get it built;

the balance would be cash at delivery." A gold plated Cadillac would be ready for Jo in about six weeks.

Back to his home, Jo started calling all his relatives, friends, neighbors and old acquaintances and told them of a perpetual party that he would start from the next day. All were welcome any time for drinks and snacks and in the evening pizzas; that was every day; he meant it. His house turned into a free restaurant and parking around his house became a problem. If any of his relatives needed any money to start a business or was in financial difficulty, he would be happy to write a check as long as it was not very close to a million dollars.

Six weeks after the order the Cadillac sales man drove gold plated Cadillac to Jo's house, and Jo wrote him a check of another $30,000. Jo was now a celebrity at his bank, in all the restaurants, bars and expensive shopping places. He would never ask how much anything would cost because he had a million dollars in his bank account. He wrote checks without figuring about the balance left in his account.

One year was not yet out since Jo won his million-dollar lottery. One morning his banker called that he had written a check that was being returned for "NOT SUFFICIENT FUNDS." Jo was furious and immediately drove to the bank and started hurling obscenities at the bank manager. He was shown more than hundred pages of his bank transactions. Jo then sensed that he was really out of his "MILLION." He drove back home, parked his Cadillac in his garage, left the loud music on, and started drinking a bottle of whisky right in the garage with the car engine running. The same evening when a lot of his "friends" came to enjoy the perpetual party, they found Jo "Departed to Heavens" with a million dollar smile.

REAL AND UNREAL SMILES

Smile research indicates, women generally smile more than men but not in all cultures and countries. In some eastern cultures laughter and smile of women is subdued. Their loud laughter is considered to be graceless and inelegant. Women are supposed to smile and laugh softly and calmly. A woman smiling at any man who does not have strong family relationship with her is frowned upon.

Smiles of American and Canadian women are omnipresent for no reason or any reason; these women can't comprehend the meaning of grace and elegance. Much of these smiling gestures are to draw attention in a company for whatever favors. These women perhaps are most liberated physically, but mentally they have enchained themselves in worst kind of liberty. Men too are in similar drain. All these smiles start decaying soon after one is over the hill of life. True real sincere love has only a literary and philosophical meaning in American life; this kind of love is incomprehensible in any highly enlightened technologically advanced culture. A real smile can't begin or survive among those who don't feel or have any attachment of souls. Great misfortune now rules the existence of millions who have all earthly possessions, but absolutely no heavenly wealth. Briefly, there are smiles of real love and there are smiles of real brutal fleeting physical pleasures.

Smile has been 'designed, crafted and fashioned' by many orthodontists. One of them theorizes about celebrity smile. This is how he correlates face shape and smile style. Oval shape is in great demand in the western world; if you are born with this shape, any orthodontic craft enhances your smile. Long faces have to contend with a horizontal line of teeth. Round faces must elongate their teeth to be attractive. If your face looks like a heart, you can't dart a smile without small teeth. A rectangular face must have rectangular teeth to carry a scented smile. Now you have assortment of designer smiles to choose from

SMILE comes in a many varieties, it can manifest itself with eyes and eyes only; this is the best manifestation of smile, for eyes can't lie. Or, it can reveal itself with full set of multicolored teeth in full view of all. Or, it can squeeze out from totally closed lips.

Or, it can just sit in the furrows of the forehead, sitting there without any good expression of the kind of smile it is or is going to be. Some can have a smile that is totally unique. Some smiles are very broad, some really narrow, some look deeply insincere and fake. A smile that a professional photographer extracts through 'cheese, cheese, cheese' is captured momentarily and does not reveal any moods in the subjects' minds. Some smiles exhibit loneliness and some too little of privacy from all around. Again, the mood behind a smile always sits in the eyes. Smile is the wordless speech that adds fragrance to speechlessness. This fragrance radiates from the face that puts it on. Say what you have to say with a smile to make yourself significantly more persuasive, pleasant, and credible.

Smile might have descended upon us from our primitiveness. It could have meant "I am happy to see you, don't attack me. Or, you are in control, I feel safe with you." The primitive meaning of a smiling face is very much alive.

Money brings about many kinds of smiles: Smile of arrogance, smile of freedom, smile of evil power, smile of putrefaction, smile of stupidity, smile of great plans and smile of outstanding achievements.

Money is the most powerful religion, life of religion and death of religion. It empowers, carries on and also kills religion. Religion has no smile ordained into it. Smile and religion have never befriended each other. Money is the cause of most crimes. It corrupts the best of minds, and bolsters the worst of minds. A corrupt person cannot wear a genuine smile.

PRAYERS FOR A SMILE

Jummu smiles whenever he claims he is a miracle of prayers. His skull that is otherwise covered with very dense short black hair, has a world-map conspicuously carved on it. He is proud to tell about the tragic accident he had some three years ago.

He was walking close to a railway track enjoying music with earmuffs. Suddenly he found himself being dragged under a train in between the railway track. The train stopped after dragging him for over 200 yards. He walked off the track with blood dripping from all over his head. When he touched his head, he did not feel any hair or skull, only some soft flesh. After that he woke up in a hospital bed some fifteen days later, fully conscious with no loss of any mental faculty. He was told that his skull was scattered all over the railway track in about 26 pieces. All the recovered pieces were sewn over his brain tissue very successfully. Now he does not even feel that he ever had this accident.

He believes only prayers are behind the miraculous recovery following the dreadful train accident. His father says that he is sure that his son is living today due to all the prayers he and all his relatives and friends all over the country made for his son. He adds that as his son was in the operating room, he called everyone he knew to go to church and pray for his son. All whom he called prayed for his son's recovery from his grave injuries.

After all the complex surgical procedures, the head surgeon informed the boy's parents that he cannot be sure of any good outcome. If their son comes out of this kind of injuries to his head and possible to brain tissues without any permanent brain damage, it will be all due to the wishes of God alone.

When after fifteen days of being in coma Jummu opened his eyes and could feel and sense all his surroundings, he asked why he was in the hospital. He had no idea of all that had happened. Jummu was then told of his dreadful accident and everything that followed it. The boy's father smiles whenever he says that he was absolutely convinced that his son was alive and fine because God listened to his prayers.

THE SMILE
OF DONE SMITH

Done Smith was the most resourceful and smiling man I encountered in my life. He took an engineering job at Chrysler after retiring as President of AM General. He was the man responsible for the design and fabrication of HUMVEE. He had changed his name from Donald Smith to Done Smith for a very good reason. His office was next to mine and I could feel he was never at rest; he was in perpetual motion. At every meeting when action items were being assigned, his response to assignments was 'CONSIDER IT DONE'. When our boss wanted to make sure a job had to be finished positively by a certain time, Done Smith was the man to receive the charge and challenge.

Done Smith was a kind of eccentric too. He owned a diabetic pug that he called Doneboy. Doneboy had a special carrier that went with Done's prize winning Harley. Doneboy was Done Smith's only companion on all vacations. Done's wife Lori, his second wife, went on vacation with her girl friends.

Once I asked Done how he became so successful and driven and why he looked like 45 at 65. He loved to tell his life story to anyone interested in listening. He started 'do you really want to know?' I responded 'yes, yes, yes!' He pulled his chair toward me, with his neck straight up and began. 'Now listen!'

"My grandparents lived at a small town in Pennsylvania in 1930s. Grandpa was a coal miner making just enough to survive. They had a little one-bedroom house where they and their six sons lived to stay alive. As any boy turned 16, he was asked to move out and find his own food and shelter. My dad, one of the six kids, did not wait until he was sixteen; he moved out when he was only 14. It took him one month to hitchhike from Pennsylvania to southern California. He was virtually illiterate and had no useful skill. A landscaper hired him and let him live in his trailer that had no water supply and toilet facility. Soon my dad was given more responsibility because he was available 24/7 for any work. He had now six men working for him. Now he thought he should get married, and he did. He married three times. He had two kids from his first wife; my sister and I; we were both lucky because our mother was very persuasive about education. Even though she had no education, she kept in touch with our school and teachers. Every day after my school I worked for at least 5 hours to supplement our income. My father left his first wife, our mother, before my sister and I were only nine and seven. It was good he left because he was not a devoted father. After my father left, he never got in touch with us.

I completed high school earning 4.00 GPA. I went for technical education. Many good schools accepted me. But I had no money and wanted to go to a university where I could get a full time night job that would pay my tuition and all other living expenses. Ohio State gave me that opportunity. All my under grad I worked 8-hour night shift and attended school in daytime hardly ever sleeping more than 5 hours a day. Close to my graduation I had many job offers. I accepted only three jobs in lifetime. I rose to presidency of AM General in less than 8 years.

My life has been only 'work'. I live, sleep, eat, drink, think and enjoy 'work'. And I call it 'A LIFE WORTH LIVING'. I cannot comprehend the concept called *retirement*. I've walked many miles of smiles after very hard early years of life. God has been kind to me, and most I came across were too."

THE SMILE
CELESTIAL OR DEADLY

Old age is destined to get us all despite all the surgical body sculpturing, medical remedies, yogic meditation, advanced nutrition and clean or dirty life styles. Each one of us shall have fake teeth, ears, and eyes to eat, hear and see with. Sleeping, eating, digesting, walking, talking, remembering, and hearing shall be a struggle. Some of us may linger for the next day in anxiety and some in peace; it shall all depend on who is waiting to receive us, God Herself or the Mother Earth.

We must praise the philosophers who invented the bright idea that life is made of an entity called soul. The soul is invisible, incorruptible and immortal, a tiny part of God Herself; it moves from one body to another, when the previous body cannot sustain it. The destiny of soul has been made a lot more complicated. It must free itself from the torture of changing its bodies; it is possible only if the human body it is in passes a sinless lifetime. This is also like an invention to control man's terrible acts. Finally, the concept of soul may be totally ridiculous, but any faith in it reduces the pain when death comes too early to those who must still live.

Life needs death because change is essential to make anything better. The present form of life, particularly human life, is full of holes and these holes have to be filled with good mortar. No matter how we slice it, at an appropriate time, death is more celestial than lethal. Considering what the poor mind, the real embodiment of life, goes through during the course of its very long journey made of sorrows and joys, health and illness, and finally imprisoned in a withered and helpless body, death should be welcome and accepted without dragging the life too long by mostly torturous means.

We have to emphasize that God and Gods are needed, they have important functions; the most important of all these functions is the one that keeps man's horrible nature under control for imaginary or real fear of hell after death. And the next important function is the consolation that we can receive from our God when we face a tragedy; this consolation is far superior to what psychotherapists and psychiatrist can provide us with after relieving our wallets of a lot of its contents. Gods have in this respect been a positive element in running a smiling life for us.

A SMILE OF POWER
Vs POWER OF A SMILE

Power takes many shapes and forms:

Power of humanity:
Of gestures, beauty,
Of love, friendship, compassion,
Of entertainment, humor
Of knowledge, imagination
Of wealth, muscles, guns
Of fear, superstition

Power of nature:
Of devastation and preservation
Of the sun, rain, wind, rivers, oceans,
Of floods, tremors, fires, lightening
Of life, death and disease
Of heavenly bodies

Every moment of life arrives with
Some vulnerability and liability
Or a kind of supremacy

Look into the power of the gun.
One who craves power of the gun,
Is an embodiment of evil,
With rare exceptions,
Power cravers are tyrants.
Their tyranny is boundless.
Tyranny does not smile,
Tyranny can't smile
For tyranny survives in frown, anger and
injustice.
All pictures, paintings and depictions of,
The cravers of power of the gun,
Wear grave and grim faces.

And power of the gun,
Is generally used to destroy,
The power of power of others.

Remember!
When you confront power of the gun,
Like or a politician in power,
An officer or petty peon of a regime,
You shall never see a smile
If you do see a smile,
It shall be only a smile of power,
A fake, cunning, and sham smile,
The most distrustful smile ever.

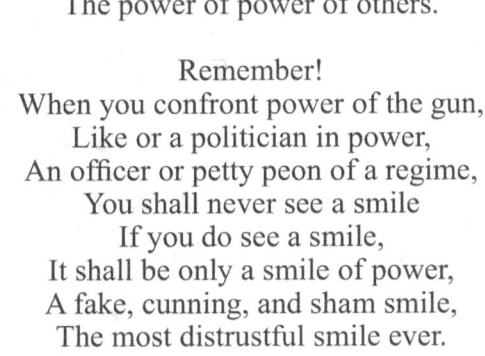

GENDERS AND SMILES

All behavioral divergences are more due to culture, age and ethnicity than due to gender. No neurological behavioral difference has been established simply based on sex.

Culture plays a strong role in behavioral patterns. All cultures all over the globe treat men and women differently. In some cultures women smile more than men, in some less and in some no difference is noticeable.

Canada and the United States are somewhat unique in the smile-culture of their populations. The whole North American excluding Mexico is of one kind; women smile more than men only among Caucasians but not among Afro-Americans. Afro-Americans laugh, smile and run their life styles with a lot less variance than other races. Age brings an immense degree of change in all behavioral patterns. There is a lot more laughter and joy in early life simply due to little stress and responsibility than when one must earn a livelihood and raise a family.

Under stress women are more tolerant than men in most cultures particularly those women who have gone through the route of motherhood. Generally, women are better humans in all aspects than men; this is perhaps a genetic trait. Women are more emotional, more soothing, more helpful, more peaceful, more harmonious, and more packed with smiles than men.

How you stand, stroll, sit, sing, dance, pray, lecture, teach, live, sleep, run, walk, talk, eat, drink, give or take, needs frames of mind, some with a lot of practice and training and some none. Smile and laughter are two activities that need no training and practice.

LET SMILES RUN YOUR LIFE

It is the law of perpetuity
No matter if times or good
Or, times are bad
The time shall not slow or stop
Nor it shall hurry or scurry
It transports fortune and misfortunes
With no passions and emotions
For some it seems fast, for some sluggish
For some it is lethargic, for some lively
Though it keeps on moving constantly
So, the wisdom of ages dictates
To run your life for success
 Wear a smile on your face

Test the power of smile
To see what it can accomplish miraculously
It is an act of joy, love, peace and all that is lovely
Go with a smile to make life less risky.
Sure remedy of all chaos is Smile therapy

Simply Smile!

To cheer up your life
Or for a friendly hike
To feel fortunate
Or light up your heart
To tell you have an easy spirit
Or make long time short
To sow a seed of goodness
Or show off your presence
To enjoy your mellowness
Or chatter in romance
To dance in harmony
Or mesmerize in mystery
To radiate your beauty
Or hypnotize your honey
If your are sad
And want to be proud
Or stand out in a crowd
To congratulate your friend
And see only good in the world
Or open up your mind
Simply smile!

ETERNAL
SMILE O'MINTS

Actions overwhelm words
Anger corrodes its container
Charisma can be cultivated
Competition is eternal
Compliment generously
Concision clears confusion
Celebrate! If you are ignorant and confident
Count your faults
Devil is in details
Don't defend your ideas
Don't sophisticate yourself
Emotional style is anemic
Enemies teach best
Face with facts
Facial-expression is 90% of impression
Flaunt arrogance humbly
Free lunch is hazardous
Freedom is not free
Genetically you are a genius
God may need you any moment
Honesty is omnipotent
Hoodwink none
Illusion-less life is life-less
Imagine freely, act in group
Inherited fortune is destructive
Laughter assaults without assaulting
Lead like a follower
Let a brief be brief
Let only love decorate your heart
Let the mind wander in wonders
Lightning works, thunder scares
Love of money is an eternal evil
Mistrust your guts
Nothing is trivial
Pessimism is potent misfortune
Prosperity can perish prosperity
Speak less, listen more
Take success humbly
Tongue is the best friend and also worst enemy
Truth can be told effortlessly

Smile is the finest ornament

THE LIFE AND DEATH OF AMBITION

There is no difference between an ambition-less mind and a lifeless mind. Luckily the mind takes birth with a blank slate, but it never dies clean. It is free to write in its book anything it desires. Ambition is the nectar the mind feeds upon. Only aspiring minds roll and reel all the humanity.

Ambition needs a seed to germinate. An atmosphere that makes one feel low, snubbed, poor, and powerless is sometimes very fertile for dreams and drives. Our familial and social umbrellas, irrespective of political and economic conditions, determine whether we are going to see the real dreams and then make them come true. We must take the settings for ambitions as part of the fate that accompanies us with the beginning of life. Random incidents do happen that agitate our minds for great beginnings. Mahatma Gandhi resolved to free his country from foreign rule only after his self-respect was seriously wounded. Abraham Lincoln rose from the pillars of poverty and humility to be one of the greatest presidents. A debilitating setback, some very bad luck, a tragedy or a huge loss can be a great booster to our will to break the barriers that stand before us to march ahead.

We see ambition thriving and decaying in every culture and country at all times. What are the common factors that give life and death to this important condition of mind?

Can we take our minds from a passive state to an active ambitious dynamism? Most likely not, for ambition only can feed ambition. However, dissatisfaction, disappointment, frustration, and similar thoughts may strengthen our drive for accomplishment.

The passage of time can make any environment acceptable to the mind, as the mind resigns and takes a permanent set to a long prevailing condition. It can and sometimes does revolt leaving serious upheavals in its own life for better or worse.

Can ambition have a spontaneous origin? The answer is in the affirmative, but the reason for the spontaneity is uncertain. We can train our minds to stay curious and be more interested in the natural world around us than in the activities of movie stars, politicians, and sports figures. Only an inquiring and learning mind can continue to be a healthy and content mind. Comparing ourselves with the accomplishments of our friends, relatives, or next-door neighbors does sometimes drive us up the ladder, but it usually happens in a stressful way. An ambition is a drive of higher and joyful order that does not care for competition; it seeks to discover the depths of the oceans, vastness of the heavens, hearts of the atoms, foundations of life, and mysteries of the mind without a competitive stress and spirit but all with smiles.

LONESOME SMILE

Year 2007, Christmas Eve, at the home of a close Lebanese friend of mine. All men and women at the party had decorated themselves in the flashiest of fashions. Everyone was wearing the best of their smiles surrounded by glittering gold, dazzling diamonds or rainbow neck-ties. Lots of cheek-rubbing, close-hugging and light kissing made a very joyful atmosphere. All the invitees were conversing in Lebanese; I could hear their laughter and see their smiles without making any sense of all that.

Somehow one very sharply dressed elderly man in his seventies came to greet me; I was thrilled to see someone interested in talking to me. He introduced himself as Kashal Habib; I could see, he wanted a soul to listen to him without interruption. He spoke very fluent Arabic laced English. I asked him how long he had been in the USA. He responded with all his life story, "I have done everything in my life; I've been a butcher, a builder, a general merchant, an importer, an exporter, a consultant, a entertainer, you name it, I've been. God has been very kind to me. I have lot more than I need. I believe in helping the less fortunate, and I have helped many."

I guessed, Kashal was a very interesting and unique personality. I interrupted him to ask him if he had any children of his own. It appeared to me, Kashal did not expect this question. He responded that he was not married and never married. He continued, " About thirty five years ago, I was at a big Lebanese cultural function in Washington, D.C. I was standing alone enjoying a drink all by myself. Suddenly I noticed a very pretty sharp girl slipped and was going to fall on her face; I rushed to hold her; I was blessed and she was lucky; she did not hit the floor, instead she was in my arms; she liked it and I was finished for life. She told me her name was Hasna. She didn't tell me that she had a law degree from an Ivy League school; I was no better than an illiterate. She did not care, she loved me and planned to spend all her life with me. Not a year went by, we were engaged. Her parents found in me a perfect match for their daughter. An elaborate wedding was planned for July 7, 1973. Just three days before the wedding day, my father called me from Beirut to give me the tragic news that my younger brother suddenly died after a short sickness. I immediately left to be by my parents. The wedding was postponed to August 26."

Now Kashal was very somber; he was remembering the long past that I could see was very fresh in his mind. He told me the rest, "when I returned from Beirut, the first call I made was to Hasna; her mother picked up the phone; I could hear her sobbing hysterically. I hung up the phone and drove straight to Hasna's home. There her father hugged me crying and told me that Hasna had a very terrible fatal car accident. Over thirty years have gone, but I feel it happened only yesterday. I believe I did marry Hasna. She has been living in my heart and mind, our smiles for each other are eternal. But I must say to the world that I am married but was never married."

The Power of Humility

Most of the harmful emotions we are prey of are innate and do not need an effort to become a part of our lives. Our evolution through uncertainties of every day, combined with fear of attacks or lack of enough food and shelter, has made us less trustful each other. We are more ready to attack and fight than solve our differences amicably. Emotions like anger, jealousy, hatred, enmity, greed, and hunger for power have been turning the wheels of our world almost continually; a day of complete peace has yet to arrive. Some of us who are socially very functional and successful lead terrible double lives. They manipulate their associates at work place, and perpetrate mental and physical abuse at home on their own spouses and children. They produce material goods and wrecked lives with equally great efficiency. They are immune to or perhaps they enjoy the emotional pain they inflict.

Under all situations, humility plays an important role not only in the state of our minds every day, but it also determines our successes and failures in the long run. At any age due to our innate nature, it affects the manner in which we are heard, received, attended by our parents, relatives, friends, bosses, subordinates, in short, everyone who interacts with us. Undoubtedly, it is a two-way street; how we are treated by and how we treat others forms our disposition. However, here we are looking into ourselves to understand that even though it is hard to be respectful to anyone who hurls an insult into our face, we would lead a happier and more successful life by returning an insult with a humble response that there appears to be some kind of misunderstanding in our tormentor's mind.

Introspection would show without much effort that no argument could be made against true humility. In some religious faiths, it is one of the essential teachings. Without it, one cannot be close to God. Life is so fragile, short, uncertain, and weak that only a fool can afford to be too sure of a future without pain and support of others. Peace has no existence without a humble atmosphere. Humility simply means treating others with respect. A humble person is not aggressive, arrogant, boastful, and vain and never resorts to anger. To her 'You before me' is a way of life. Anger kills friendships and marriages. Resentments ruin families and associations. Prejudice builds walls between religions. Malicious gossip destroys peace and joy. Greed can never bestow lasting prosperity. Wars begin with humiliating arrogance.

Humility has been asserted to be one of the very important virtues in most of the religions. It is the mother of peace and harmony. It elevates our worth in the eyes of others. We are trusted more if we are humble. If we want to truly lead, humility has to be the horse pulling the carriage on which we all can ride as equals. No great leadership can begin or survive without humility. All wars begin in anger and end in humility; it is learning the hard way.

FREEDOM IS NOT FREE

Freedom was never free
And shall never be free
Indeed, freedom is an illusion

First, freedom has to be willed
Then it has to be defended
And has to be secured
Finally, it has to be preserved

Defense, security and preservation of freedom
Require blood, sweat and sacrifice
Of life, time and wealth
Without pause and breather
From the nefarious acts of
The ruler, freedom's true executioner

No one is born free
For birth is bound by genes
Childhood is bound by parental constraints
Parenthood is bound by broods
Education is bound by rigid rules
Adulthood is bound by rigorous restraints
Livelihood is bound by employers
Love is bound by cultural rules
Youth is bound by aging
Life is bound by disease
Time is bound by destiny
Death is bound by time

Hunger and thirst rules
From birth to death
Desire knows no ends

Truly
No one can live free
No one has lived free
No one dies free
No one can die free

Of all the possessions
If anything is free
It is only a SMILE
It is evocative and convincing
It is persuasive and crushing
It is the real and true power
And it is free forever

Without emotions we would be like a robot. We need emotions to feel alive, to enjoy life, to love and be loved, to have a purpose in life and to do whatever it takes to defend ourselves when danger lurks around the corner. Emotions are as responsible for good health as for debilitating diseases. They can build or destroy our lives. Emotions of hate and enmity ignite wars that kill millions, and those of clean self-interest generate everlasting prosperity. There is emotional attachment and emotional detachment; we need both in the right proportions to run our lives properly lubricated.

A SMILE IS NOT AN EMOTION
but it is the outburst, representation
and eruption
of the best of all emotions
-HAPPINESS-

SMILE ALIVE

John was a sales executive of a big manufacturing company. He visited me at least once a month to keep me informed of new products. He would normally come to see me just before lunch time, and would ask me if I would be kind enough to go with him for a bite. We would spend over one hour enjoying food and pleasant atmosphere. John enjoyed drinking and massive steaks; he always had three to four orders of hard liquor; never wine or beer. Strangely enough his physiology did not show any sign of drunkenness; his tolerance level by virtue of his genes was exceptionally high.

John wore a kind of perpetual smile. Every part of his face, his eyes, forehead, lips, chin and down to the middle of his neck appeared joyful and radiated happiness. He had nothing to criticize nothing, as the saying goes. He was tall, attractive and on heavy side, and loved to eat, talk, listen and laugh. Over a period of fifteen years I met him at least hundred times and enjoyed his company. He had many funny and interesting tales to tell. I could see that all his colleagues were very happy with him. Near the end of my association with John, I saw him loosing quite a bit of fat and also fashioning a well trimmed artistic beard. I told him he looked sharper in his new attire. He smiled and said he was following his doctor's advice. He visited me four or five times after he wore a beard, and every time he was leaner. His smile did not change a bit.

It was a nice sunny Friday, John visited me. We went to lunch. He told me he would let me know the coming Monday when my order could be shipped. His smile was no different from what it was when I saw him the first time so many years ago. I expected a call from John the Monday morning. Not hearing anything from him, I called his office in the afternoon. It was John's boss who gave me the painful news that John passed away on Saturday just a day ago. I was shocked and surprised and asked what happened. He told me John was suffering from terminal liver cancer for the last one year; he worked up to the last breath of his life. I went to John's funeral. John was lying there in this casket with a natural peaceful smile still radiating from his face hiding behind a well trimmed beard. There were close to a thousand mourners to honor John at the end of his journey, many of them crying and sobbing. The funeral procession was over a mile long. Smile was ingrained in John's face. It was still there when his soul had left his mortal body. A smile alive it was.

THE FRAME THAT SMILES SUPREME

The brain is the abode of the mind, and the mind is the embodiment of thoughts. The scientific observation that brain and mind die simultaneously is irrefutable; why one never survives the other has many philosophical explanations. Where in the brain the mind parks itself is the subject of greatest vigor among the most ambitious researchers. The brain is more intricate than the universe and the mind exceeds the brain in complexity. Billions of neurons and trillions of synapses keep on firing, acting, reacting, storing, and communicating to and from sensory organs as long as the structure of the brain is not damaged, diseased, or dead. The most advanced methods for imaging the biological state of the brain can only show us the patterns of blood flow to its various sectors and any variations of it from the normal anatomical shape. We do know almost precisely which parts of the brain communicate with which sensory organs, e.g., eyes, ears, tongue, nose, and skin. But we do not know how all the neurochemicals convert the material stuff of the brain to the awareness called 'I', 'ME', 'SHE' or 'YOU'. We should accept the fact that the evolution process has not yet given the brain the ability to comprehend itself.

From the very moment a human infant is freed to breath by herself, her mind starts building a frame that increases in rigidity as time goes by. Sooner than later, by the time she enters into her teens, the frame takes the final form, and the foundation of her life is pretty well set. What she hears, tastes, sees, or is made to see, taught or not taught, given to or taken from, how she is hated or loved, the way she is spoken to, the way her words are rejected or accepted, how she is permitted to exhibit herself in speech or person to her parents, friends, teachers and relatives determine what she would like, hate, fear, love, desire, hope for, accept, or reject all through the rest of her life unless she is fortunate enough to stray into a great deal of such knowledge that will open the knots of her aged mental frame and replace them with new ones. This change can come if she can muster a lot of discipline and determination and she is willing to take a lot of risk - a hard but possible task.

Smile does not only make the face more pleasant to look at, but also tells the brain to make endorphin. Endorphin is the biochemical that reduces both physical and emotional stress and fosters joy and happiness.

Smile, the power of this sweetest of all gestures, is underestimated. It is like a speechless acceptance of other person's pleasant presence. Some simple facts are irrefutable; stomach throws up when we down into it any concoction that it does not want to accept; unfortunately the mind has quite a dangerous way of treating what it finds obnoxious. We only have to make a sincere effort to guard our brains from poisonous ingredients taking hold of them and we then can go up the road to a live a smiling life that we find relaxing and enjoyable.

Facial expressions are vastly dependent upon the immediate surrounding social or business environment. Imagine a gorgeous woman being in the sight of a handsome man opposed to being observed by only another attractive woman. A mother watching her own playful baby will carry a smile, but all alone she may be walking around with a long face.

People monitor their own personality for best impressions when being monitored for any kind of performance.

Smile is meditation, contemplation and reflection of the best elements of human nature. The real good world is made of smiles and laughter. No peace is possible without understanding and practicing these two elements.

SMILE SPROUTS CHEERFULNESS AT HOME, PROMOTES FRIENDLINESS IN A BUSINESS AND SPRINGS PEACE IN THE MIND.

SMILE DOES NOT HAVE TO BE BOUGHT, ASKED FOR, LOANED, STORED IN A BOX OR PRESERVED. IT IS AVAILABLE ANY MOMENT WHEN AN ATMOSPHERE OF JOY IS TO BE CELEBRATED.

SMILE IS A SPIRITUAL SUTRA FOR THE SOUL. IT SWEETENS WITHOUT SUGAR, SOOTHES WITHOUT CREAM AND FEEDS WITHOUT ANY FOOD.

BOOZED-UP SMILE
A BOOZER'S MONOLOGUE

Thank You, God!
For making me of human brand
And for giving me a confused mind
I had babyhood packed of pleasure
But as I grew into adolescence in leisure
The sparkles of life started to departure

Then as years went by my enthusiasm
I was assaulted by strange destitution
My soul immersed in a bizarre pollution
Friends I had many, but I don't fathom
What they were, or what I was to them

You gave me a musical mind
A gene to love and be loved
Intellect to amuse and be amused
Also foolhardiness to be destroyed
By a lot of stuff of dreadful kind

You granted me all the ingredients
To kill boredom by many means
Sunrise, sunset, sunshine, rainbows
Flowers, canyons and mountain peaks
Colorful birds singing their songs
And also some terrible fangs
To wreck Your beautiful creations

Adore someone close or distant
For boredom never to confront
If friends can treat or cure monotony
Then you don't need gin or whiskey
Also rum, vodka, Irish cream or brandy

When a sip of scotch slips down my
esophagus
A million blissful slivers go up my spinal
column
Through the spine the bliss is harbored in
my skull

The skull wherein the I of me is said to
dwell
Much of scotch slowly wrecks my liver
My kidneys also face a dangerous enemy
When boozed, I feel like a dutiful donkey
But as potent as a commander-in-reality
Vodka empowers me to feel trustworthy
Believe me you, then very honestly
Good and bad look all illusory

Whiskey makes me beautifully raised
Gin churns me up sharply talented
Boozed up, I don't feel disoriented
But with a soul baffled and lubricated
I gain confidence though fully bewildered
They claim, boozing is dreadful and
wicked
But I claim this remedy dances in my mind

A real camel can work seven days without
eating
A real man can eat seven days without
working

But a boozed man can consume whole
life drinking

If you are shrewd, dose to obsession
To unite with God with passion
Not much you can do to comprehend
Because everyone is slave of likelihood

Champagne: A celestial thirst-quencher
Now the unanimous canon of celebration
The only source of excellent exuberance
An indispensable feature of feasting
To lay an evil eye on a pretty thing

I discovered miracles of vodka!
It was in the dead cold of Alaska
I felt as if I was in a wild mazurka
If you are lucky to start with Gin
You have good plan for the life to begin
Polluting all your hemoglobin

The best of all is brandy
If you crave to be somebody
With a soul totally moody
And a brain that is truly cloudy
To feel like a chairman or chair lady

From heavens, they say came whisky
To give men of God a thing very spooky
And cheapest apparatus for infertility
Sooner or later, trust me you junky
Between your legs you shall be a leaky

Boozed up I feel I'm in paradise
And as free as the USA
To do what I please with a smile
Boozer, a good boozer I've been for
a long while
Truly, this is how I wear a
perpetual smile

GOD's HEAVENLY ABODE

God's crucial inquest into Her universe
From Her eternal vastness of cosmos
A splendor of gigantic magnificence

Oh Humans!

Of the universe I'm the Supreme Creator
Omnipotent and Omniscient Originator

In umpteen words you have Me labeled
Finally you coined "Grand Old Dad", God!
Material obsessions of life is your only end
That in all facets is too sad

You are My most ingenious playthings
Bestowed upon to peer into My mysteries
And to have an inkling of My secrets
You are on a luxuriant planet to multiply
But you shall never grasp the Almighty
Go, as deep as can, it never shall be profound
In truth and reality, for you to comprehend

Your main conjectures are worthless
Since the universe is purposeless
It didn't have to come into existence
I created it to veil in it My Omnipotence

You can't realize
To plan the universe
TIME is the most complex element
I had to create for motion to transpire
For, without TIME motion is not viable
And without motion, no change is possible
The universe needed TIME to be conceived
And thereafter to change and expand

Don't forget, TIME is supreme
You are born, age, reborn and heal
In the realm of TIME to reconcile

Few of you know the real thing
That the only thing you know
Is that you know nothing
Let it be to you very soothing
I have not given you the faculty
To sense the meaning of reality

To be able to take a peek into one's own soul is a thorny task. If you can honestly believe that you do not harbor any ill-will against anyone, you may celebrate your humility. You may then look into a mirror and sincerely smile at your greatest achievement.

Smile may not be evolutionary, although the theory of evolution may hold some water. Many a time smile is less joyful to the smile-giver than to the smile-receiver. For the simple reason, that a smile can be so effortlessly faked, it can be argued that the creation of smile is as mysterious as life is. Smile is a sign of kindness, symbol of love, figure of good impression, image of simplicity, indication of closeness, representation of peace, mark of humility, character of goodness, and a badge of secret sweetness.

SMILE OF AN APE

Oh God!

Are you really proud?
Of Your contraption? Called man!
Your ingenious formation!
You needed him, for what reason?

And Oh God!
I can see plainly, but why You don't
What a plunderer, Your man has been
From the very time, You gave him that big brain

He destroys his own kind for exuberance
And has gone on many a murderous rampage
He has imaged You in many a frame
And that too to wage wars in Your name
That also without any shame

Why did You make his brain so squirmy
At all the places and all the times he is fidgety
Every moment of his life he on attack
For his immense love of greenback

Tell me, why You took man's tail away
A tail would have made him less phony
Why you made him walk on only two
If he too walked on his four
He would be less sour

Listen, Oh God!
I honor your creation, I live and let live
My smile is true and never deceptive
It is never fake or tart
For You have given me a kind heart

Hard work may take You from here to there A smile will take You everywhere

Smile being an important element of human body language has been researched into from a million diverse viewpoints. Humans have not been shaped like trees to stand at a point and do the talking. Both sexes want to exhibit their burrows, furrows, toughness, eloquence, expressiveness, persuasiveness, vigor and all that agreeable stuff. Except for geniuses, talking is a crucial segment of success and failure in life. Here is body language philosophized. Liars smile with smile-less eyes. If eyes smile too long, it is either for true deep love or for a show of flirting. A smile with your hands behind your back is only a sign of arrogance due to whatever motive. Smile is an infant's first stage of body language, and apparently related to nothing; after a few months the smile becomes social because it is given to a familiar face. Happiness always rides a carriage decorated with smiles. A fast talking smiling salesperson is out to get you. So one must learn how to grade a smile.

THE SMILESHIP

In a large housing development I had a simple little apartment to live at for a few years. The architects and landscapers planned this project beautifully and imaginatively. They left some tracks of land in total natural setting. A twisted and curly lake surrounded by a wide pedestrian walk sat right in the center of many apartment buildings. My apartment was everyday visited by sunrise and sunset when clouds were not in the way. I strolled around the curly lake every morning and evening during summer months. I could find more peace emanating from the lake, shrubs and trees standing by the water, ducks and swans swimming by the waves and wind and breeze, than any imaginable invention or discovery made by man.

One summer I saw an elderly couple – most probably husband and wife – taking leisurely walks every morning and evening around this heavenly lake. They walked with most harmonious smiles next to each other never at any perceptible distance. Two white poodles they had were always either pulling them or they had to pull them to keep them by their side. The poodles walked, ran, stopped, jumped all in harmony, as if there was no fun better than that. And they appeared to me happier in each other's company than any pair of human beings I have ever met. Often I bumped into this couple; they would greet me and I would smile, stop and talk to them about their life experiences. I asked them about their poodles and how long they had this pair. The poodles were old and did not have much time left, I was told.

Three months went by and I saw these "four" every day. One evening when I was out a little early, I saw this elderly couple walking with only with one poodle. I asked the lady where is the other poodle. She responded tearfully "two days ago he died of old age and since then the living poodle had not eaten anything; he would not come for a walk; we too are very depressed to see our baby so lonely."

A few days later, I met this couple around the lake sitting and crying on a bench without their second poodle. I could sense that the second poodle just could not survive without his companion.

The couple was not in the best of health. They did not have much time left. They were significant company of each other. I did not see them with any other human being. Poodles were their pastime that was now gone. I did not see much of them after the poodles. One day there was some commotion around where they lived – an ambulance and fire truck. I hurried over and was told that the old man was gone. I attended the funeral; the lady dressed in finest of clothed stood crying at the casket. Not much is left that I can now tell.

A week later the elderly woman left this world to be with her companion in God's abode.

How do I wonder and wander!
I have asked this question of many "if you had to choose between the following TWO offers:

1. The most magnificent palace located at the best scenic place in the world surrounded by the greatest variety of beautiful flowery plants, trees and colorful singing birds, with all imaginable worldly comforts, best of foods, hundreds of kingly or queenly wardrobes --- but, but, but absolutely NO loving human companionship, contact and interaction.

And

2. A simple hut with a door and roof, located at a dry and desolate land, with little physical comfort and nature's raw food--- but, but, but a loving human companionship, contact and interaction. "
What would you choose?

The answer has always been the later.
Companionship – a loving companionship – has no substitute – shall never have a substitute. This is all that is needed to run a smiling life. Rest all is in superfluous and meaningless.
And that is the only philosophy of life THAT MATTERS.

The state of mind is all that life is made of. It is this state that affects not only our mental peace but also our physical health. Many research studies have shown that the time it takes for a simple ailment like cold and cough to a complex life- threatening disease like cancer to go through the course of treatment and cure depends greatly on how and what a patients thinks of her body in an unhealthy condition. Mental stress is the phrase used for undesirable component of the state of mind; this stress has now been found to worsen many disease-producing conditions. Diminished infection fighting ability, toxic metabolism, elevated blood pressure, weakened heart muscles, malfunctioning digestive system, ulcerated mucous intestinal lining, reduced blood supply to brain, loss of memory due to lack of concentration, more frequent allergic reactions, and higher rate of depression are some of the effects of mental stress. Every act of life can be eased and smiled at to keep the mind healthy and in peace.

SMILE OF LOVE

Love, next to livelihood, dominates life. The more disposable time we have the more kinds of loves more often and with more tangles we engage in. A loveless smile is never a real smile.

Love can be seen as the nectar of life. How dry would life be without this lively emotion! Without any attachment, without any deep feeling for someone or something, life would feel very purposeless. However, when we go into the details of this godly and devilish emotion, we shall find that love needs many limits to its expression and practice. At times, it fills us with intense joy and at times, with unbearable pain.

Briefly, love is a synonym for mental attachment and is only about attempting to possess, being in possession of, or being possessed by someone or something. We could be in love with our bodily attributes, children, parents, siblings, friends, houses, trees, collectables, pets, money, fame, power, jobs, Gods, religions, leaders, followers, hobbies, country, race, and so on. Intensity and duration of all this love varies. Some of this love is reciprocated and some not, and our happiness, relaxation, and even depth of sleep are dependent on the responses we receive from those we love.

Quality of life is a fashion talk among the educated and sophisticated. Ordinary people discuss life in different words. However, we can assign an index of misery and joy to the state of our minds. The more unsatisfied wants and needs we have, the higher is our misery index, the greater the satisfaction, the higher the joy index. Love, in one form or other, is at the base of quality of life.

It is egoistic and spiritual snobbery to claim that one is free from love of money or the things money translates into.

Love has two origins – innate and cultivated. For one's child, it is innate; for one's country, it is cultivated. Love that leads to the perpetuation of species is unique and is really a kind of attachment with weak and temporary links, and should be appropriately called fleshy love.

It is the fleshy love that havocs many lives in many different ways. Mother Nature is most selfish in this regard, because in her mind no sacrifice is too big for the next generation to start and grow.

The gravitational attraction, the sensual feelings, the poetic creations, the romantic dances and dinners, the seduction by perfumes, the crushing crush, the imaginations and longings of the innocent hearts, command all pairs of lovers to fall into the valley of fleshy love in complete disregard of any deadly dangers to health, prohibiting laws and cultural mores and also despite every incompatibility in their personalities.

After the lovers climb out of their valleys of love, they see how different they are from each other. When they break up or divorce, they use every weapon to protect the product of their love, but at the same time they try their best to annihilate each other.

Loneliness, truly, is non-existent. One is always in the company of one's own thoughts and reflections. All that keeps on going in the brain's zillions of cells can be tortuous or joyous. Whatever is in the view of eyes at any moment can't be ignored by the almighty mind. Joy is in the mind of the observer is as true as *the beauty is in the eyes of the beholder*. For some the sky is blank and for some it is the most beautiful wonder to wonder and smile about every moment of life.

Smile mends shattered connections, fixes hard feelings, restores warmness, heals pain and repairs broken hearts.

Smile is an instrument of persuasion. It weakens disagreements, diminishes human distances, and strengthens your point of view.

Smile is a mighty means of interaction, but insignificantly exploited. No joy, happiness, great emotions, true companionship and sincere care can be expressed without a sincere smile.

Smile carrying person is watched and envied. A smiling person is considered to be successful, cooperative, helpful, approachable and open-minded.

Smile walks through telephone lines and space-waves to cause favorable responses without any images and pictures. It can be felt and detected by the person on the receiving end.

A DRINK FOR A SMILE

Tender loving care
Is Nature's true character

She concocted alcohol
The very real cocktail

Fast formula for fun
If a life needs nothing done

When the brain is empty
A drink imbues this cavity

The love of rich and poor
A drink is skull's best collaborator

Drink and drive to kill somebody
And cripple twice as many

When you are lonely
Walk into a bar ecstatically
To be robbed and fleeced joyfully

To thrill body and heart
Alcohol is the head honcho
To rule the very essence of soul

Life, without it, is a piece of crap
The truth is passed down
From generation to generation
Very proudly without intermission

To destroy
Your descendants and tranquility
And past, future, love and harmony

So, drink for a smile
To feel proud in the hell

THE SMILE OF BOREDOM

Boredom is a potent power
And it is omnipresent
It is blankness of a blank brain
And it can make you miserable
You may be a bore
Or you may be a dazzling bore
You may be living in a crowd of bores
Or you may be burdened by boredom
Simply, it is plainly a state of mind
And is a cause of abundant depression
Alcohol and many other drugs suppress it
But alcohol is the remedy of choice
In every corner and nook of the world
To numb, dull and freeze the brain
And also to celebrate short lived elation

In fact, boredom gains strength
As brain builds immunity
To the very agents that are supposed to perish it
Alcohol was not a discovery or an invention
Mother Nature's kingdom had it all planned
Through natural fermentation of fruits
Without this stuff life would be a tragedy
Wonder, as it goes down the throat
A miracle ought to happen
And a miracle sure does

A drunk suddenly becomes open, social and submissive
Mentally weak, elevated, talkative, emotionally unstable,
Poor in perception, comprehension and visual sharpness

But, without a drink, life is empty
So, drink, Oh man, drink!
God designed boredom for some good purpose
Along with all its negatives
Boredom is necessary for people to be friendly and social
And for people to smile at each other
Long live boredom!

Smile is one great method for listening more and talking less. It is like a nod, affirmation, go-ahead for telling the talker that the listener is sincere and interested in whatever is being said.

Smile is a means for deep relaxation. Just watching a cloudy and thundering sky, a dark starry night, a bright sunny day or any wonder of nature with a smile brings about to the material brain a kind of peaceful contentment.

Smile is an important hullabaloo of the complex nervous network. It orders the network to glow the face, lips and face with the message that it is happy with whatever is around.

Smile has gone through a long process of evolution. Smile mixed with bashfulness is a sign of grace and beauty in the cultures where open closeness between two sexes is frowned upon. This smile is absent from the 'advanced' cultures. This is the smile of true and deep love. This is the smile that can't be faked.

Smiles of very early years of life, in a baby crib, in kindergarten, in an elementary school and then middle school and high school grow into happy life in adulthood. Many studies show mind is kind of programmed into elation by the settings of very young years of life.

Smiles are divided into two genders, like the rest of all life, male and female. Male smile differs from female smile in sharpness, fakery, broadness, timing, duration and age. Cultural pounding play important role in how smile is displayed by females and males in various countries and cultures. Education, professions and financial status all enforce their forces on the form and kind of a smile.

HOW TO BE! ON TOP OF THE WORLD!

Arise early
Begin dynamically
Choose cautiously
Defend strongly
Earn honestly
Forgive heartily
Give meekly
Grow brilliantly
Help graciously
Judge precisely
Laugh heartily
Lead humbly
Learn enthusiastically
Listen attentively
Live cheerfully
Love truthfully
Marry faithfully
Move attentively
Munch sparingly
Plan carefully
Praise genuinely
Serve wholeheartedly
Socialize respectfully
Speak sweetly
Take gratefully
Talk serenely
Think rationally
Wait patiently
Walk briskly
Work industriously
Worship devotedly

And most importantly Smile sincerely

Smile always keeps many doors open for you wherein you are welcome. Who does not want to associate with happiness!

Smile implies happiness. Smile! and the world shall smile with you; frown! and you shall have no company.

Smile can be thought to be a duty and obligation that one owes to the world for being born on this beautiful planet.

If you are too busy to smile, your joy is in a collapsing style.

The concept *peace of mind* was discovered by some Indian and Chinese philosophers. The Western world borrowed only a component of peace from the East not too long ago. All the research on mental stress is about lack of tranquility, peace and simplicity in our lives.

This *peace* is the piece that makes life worth living
LIVING WITH A SMILE

The face speaks without speaking the story of the body it hangs on and the mind it is commanded by. And a face with a smile tells that the heart, it is alive due to, has been living a smiling life.

LOVE AND SMILE

This cuddled baby and cuddling mom are more happy and content than any humans can ever imagine. They are not worried about the next moment, next day or next year for any reason.

Each and every feature, function, process, change, growth and decay, birth, aging and end of life is planned, designed and executed by the almighty DNA. A man and a monkey are equally impotent before its supremacy.

Oh humans!

Take a lesson from these purest and simplest of souls. The innocence, selflessness, love and devotion for each other, this beautiful pair of God's creation radiates is pure and powerful.

Look, look beyond yourself to make someone else smile, it takes only little effort.

Be happy and smile for the simple reason that you can prepare and plan for anything that may go wrong the next moment, next day or next year. In this matter only you may feel that you are a little better than a monkey.

SMILE, THE COSTUME

One fine beautiful morning, in a mansion style home, a woman opens her bathroom door and finds her man standing in front of the bathroom mirror. She looks into the mirror and finds her man standing facing the mirror. His eyes are without doubt closed. How puzzling it is to her, how mysterious! She touched her man's shoulder tenderly and asks what the mirror is doing for him, if he has his eyes closed.

The man responds, my love, I wish to know how I look to you when I am asleep.

And you know, I want you to see me happy when I am with you, awake or asleep. The woman is ecstatic and promises to herself that she will never wear a face that does not look beautiful to her love. So she asks him how she can look beautiful to him every moment, every hour of every day.

Her man is overjoyed to hear this, smiles and replies, Love, you look to me beautiful, truly, most beautiful When you wear a smile for me that is all you need as your costume.

IN LOVE, IT IS TRUE
A SMILE CHASES YOU
WHEREVER YOU GO

Love, to be free of fears
And also to drench in tears

For everything there is a reason
But not for love, if looked with precision

Love is the light less flame
In which to enjoy the divine game

Don't just fall in love, crumple in it
Once you get soaked, you shall discover
What it means to be a pauper

Love's gravitation can pull any heart
Love speaks a little and listens a lot

Be a prisoner of love to feel free
And to live a life on an apple tree

Love is soul's real function
And life's only admiration

A looser in love is always a winner
Keep on losing and be a pioneer

Ageing crawls in love, not in vain
Pang of love is the divine pain

Love is a song without words
Also the universal solution of all troubles

Love is the universal therapy
For every allergy

Love is a superb therapeutic drug
Forever, be in love to feel young

Love radiates powerful fragrance
And empowers your prominence

Love is the best version of life
That too, before life and afterlife

So, in love
A smile chases you
Wherever you go

FAMILY IN THE REAL SMILE

Only the fortunate ones smile with a family, continue with a family and shall end with a family.

Most of us believe that we belong to a family of some kind, small or big, good or bad, broken or well-knit, helpful or selfish, and so on. The most common and restricted meaning of the word family has been a set of mother, father and their own unmarried and financially dependent children; as soon as a child gets married, she is said to have her own family.

Culturally speaking, the depth and breadth of a family may vary from a two-member unit to over twenty members, and feelings of the members for each other could also be very different in different cultures; wealth and poverty also alter the feelings in the long run.

The family a child was reared in determines the kind of an adult that emerges from the body and mind of that child. Right from the moment an infant begins to breath of her own, her mind for the first decade of her life experiences an exponential growth not in the physical size but in the amount of observations and experiences retained. The role that a child's family plays in molding her future far exceeds the impression made by all rest of the environment created by the society, the culture and the country she is born in. How we are raised by our parents or guardians in our early childhood determine to the largest degree the kind of behavioral and moral foundation we would stand on. This foundation is more like the mental fortune that we inherit and it shapes our minds a lot more powerfully than the material fortune that is passed on to us to live a life of smile.

To begin a dialogue
The first word that one must speak
Is the word that is not spoken
For it is the word called smile
Any talk that begins with a smile
Is an exchange of beliefs
That is bound to end in deals

To live with confidence
Keep a smiling appearance
You are the only hindrance
If you can't find any romance

Smile lies exactly
In the middle
Of simplicity
And harmony

Smile, joy and happiness are perpetually floating around us. These elements of ecstasy are as omnipresent as God. They gurgle in every particle, pebble, stream, snow-flake, lightning, rain-drop, sunrise, sunset….

And, the sight and touch of every fruit and flower leaves a very soothing smile in our souls.

Smile and success are strongly related. Just as it is better to be rich than poor, it is better to be happy than unhappy and it is better to smile than frown. Somehow happy people are cooperative and motivating. One of the reasons of being fired is noncooperation with coworkers. Smile is a source of engagements and connections. Too much of a smiling face will annoy not too many people. There is no smooth road to smooth life, but there is a smooth life on a smiling road.

LET THE LUCK SMILE

Our lives roll on a set of three mismatched wheels right from the first day of our birth. Fortune, fate and luck are these wheels. Fortune locks in at the moment of birth; fate is the environment that an individual can hardly change; luck is the random unprejudiced stroke that ruins or rewards poor and rich, week and strong without any discrimination. Present is infinitesimally short, past and future infinitely long. The past cannot be altered, and the future is unknown. The past cannot be lived in, but it is our constant companion, as we see, it very significantly determines what our future may be.

The expertise for predicting the future has always been in great demand and the sophistication of the methods to satisfy the hunger to know the tomorrow has followed the technology. The moment and location of birth of each one of us is unique in reference to stars and our solar system, and so the astrologers claim that our destiny is determined at the very moment we step into the world and is unalterable, no matter what. Astrologers and their astrology have been in demand since the dawn of humanity and nothing appears to wane it. Many kings, queens, emperors, and also chief politicians-in-command of the modern era have trusted the stars of their birth to commence auspicious beginnings of their reigns and ravages. The amusing and amazing fact is that it is impossible to show that a prediction is ever true, because there is no telling that what occurred at a given moment was really supposed to occur.

Many of us are willing to give up a fortune to know with certainty what the rest of our lives hold for us. We have not really pondered upon our desire and need to bear up all the surprises that are waiting for us for all the years to come. If our future sits before us with an open book, and we find a very tragic event coming down upon us whether tomorrow or thirty years hence, we could fall into severe melancholy or depression; and if a moment of immense joy is in the waiting, the knowledge of it will take away most of the joy from the joy of it. It may be difficult to comprehend that a book on our future will be the greatest tragedy that would fall upon us; we should not ask for it, possess it, or see it, if we want to enjoy the moment we are at.

Let the future be uncertain! Keep on smiling and let the luck strike as it may. It is the most desirable way of leading a life.

KEEP ON SMILING!
THE ALMIGHTY LUCK
IS IN COMMAND

If a lottery strikes, it could be the beginning of many joys or sorrows; when lightning strikes, it could be the end of them all. We move around randomly and so does luck, and meeting of the two at the right time and right place or at the wrong time and wrong place can make us cry or laugh, sometimes all of our lives.

On the tragic side, highly sophisticated flying machines do crash. Bridges wash away the moment before trains or buses are about to cross. Drunk drivers are free to smash head-on and turn some the best of us into paraplegics. One of the thousands of arteries in our brains abruptly decides to leak. Genes we inherit suddenly wake up and hit us with a brain tumor. An attack by some hitherto unknown virus or bacteria ends our dreams forever. Police chasing a fleeing felon send innocent pedestrian flying thousands of feet away to her death. On the lucky side, we miss our confirmed reservation flight that crashes, killing everyone on board. The doctor catches the malignancy in our throat before it becomes untreatable. We buy a run-down stock and then sell it at its peak just before it goes down the drain.

The almighty luck would keep us wondering all over. How do we comprehend, control, or tame it? Good luck! He was just lucky. Luck really saved her. Always believe in luck. No matter how hard you work, only luck would decide. We cannot see the future, and we should neither attempt to see it for the life to stay as a surprising revelation. We can make a reasonable assessment of terrible or terrific happenings in the next moment or on the next day and still find that we were totally wrong.

THE COMMAND OF LUCK!
I'm in control. Don't ever lose your smile now or for the next moment.

Love is true beauty
True beauty love
That is all ye need know
Open arms and open smile
Manifests beauty and love

Oh humans!

Ponder seriously!

You are the most dangerous of all the creatures my God has crafted for my planet. From the day you come down from the heavens to the last moment you are called back, you keep your body and mind engaged in adulteration, destruction, pollution and mutilation of all the magnificence my God has created.

You decorate your exterior with gold, diamonds and jewels, but your interior smolders with greed and gluttony.

Do not clothe me for your fascinations and destroy the smile of my heart. If you let me live the way God wanted me to, you shall wear a happy smile on your exterior and in your heart too.

SMILE OF KARMA

Karma is a Sanskrit word that means an intentional mental or physical act. 'Karma Yoga', a Sanskrit phrase, means a path of union through action. In this aspect of life one must conduct oneself without being attached to the outcomes of one's deeds. All deeds should aim at achieving the Supremacy of God.

The acceptance and practice of yoga has been growing in the western world for quite some time. Only a very miniscule component of yoga has been understood, and the practice in the west is mostly for physical flexibility and fitness. In fact, the meaning of yoga has been distorted and diminished. From the very beginning the primary purpose of yoga has been to discipline the process of thinking and to channel the power of mind. Realizing deeply that no accomplishment is possible without good health, working for physical fitness is only the secondary purpose of yoga. Total practice of yoga integrates mental and physical well-being. To come to the final form of the principles, divisions, and methods of practice of the variety of yoga known today took the inventive sages hundreds of years.

We want here to go into the depths of only Karma Yoga, also called the Law of Karma. In a very indirect way, this yoga delves into the forces of luck by telling us that our plan may not go by our plan and we should therefore do just what is essentially good and virtuous. What our well-intended actions are going to result in is barely in our control.

No matter what religious faith we wish to govern ourselves by, or whether we fancy an undisciplined and free mind, we feel unhappy or dejected to varying degrees if our labor does not reward us with the fruits we expected. It is difficult for us to visualize the part all the factors and variables play in the outcome of any action.

Convincing has proven to be easy if gods did the convincing, so gods were made to give birth to the fundamental morality. Due to its immense importance a god is made to explain the meaning of Karma Yoga in Hindu scriptures; the humans are mortal, weak, and shall never be capable to account for all the unknowns that determines the finality. So a god teaches a devotee that humans must take an active path to truth, selflessness, and freedom. To do the right thing and not wait for or expect any results is the essence of Karma Yoga or Law of Karma.

The foundation of the Law of Karma is eternal. Life can be run well, if we realize that all actions have consequences. We may hide from the punishment accorded by man-made laws, but our rebirth will be associated with outcomes of all our virtues and vices in this life. Genetically, this doctrine makes a lot of sense. We are closely linked to our ancestors, and our descendents will carry a mixture of our genes; this process could be called reincarnation. May be the sages did mean what the latest genetic research has found, but they expressed their philosophy in a more convincing language coming from the mouth of a god.

The tales of ills of large inheritances or expectation thereof are many and new ones are in the news all the time. The larger the inheritance, the greater the chances of low moral character of the heirs, family feuds, enmity, distrust, and hypocritical relationships. When empires are waiting to be inherited, the lives of the reigning emperors and kings are not safe even from their own offspring; our history speaks of many powerful dynasties that witnessed imprisonment, torture or murder of emperors by their own sons when the thrones were about to be passed on.

Dynasties of the rich decay whilst the descendents of the poor and the middle class ascend to prosperity and power. The cycle of riches to rags, and rags to riches is perpetual but the repeat time runs into many generations, and therefore, not noticeable by one particular generation to motivate itself to change its course of action from going down the drain. Karma smiles with its omnipotent reach sometimes in one's own life and mostly in one's descendants' lives.

THE SMILES OF LUCK

The past ought to convince us with a smile that we should let chance enjoy the liberty that she has ordained for herself. We can take any chunk of time, small or big, and shall find that planning for the future works sometimes and but does not most of the times. More than three-fourths of all new ventures fail. Most of us work hard to excel, the rest of us, simply to end up in the middle of the road. Mediocrity should not be called mediocrity, because it is more like the basic rule of the Providence. Like statistical normal distribution of the quality of all technological products that we turn out, humans are cultivated by their environment such that more dissimilarity goes with smaller population. This means that no matter how hard we try; only a small fraction of all endeavors is going to result in great successes or terrible failures.

Many real life examples abound, from the long past to the very recent times, to prove that life is like an intricate game of cards. Wisdom is to understand it, manipulate it whenever we can, and accept it with grace when we cannot. We spend more time competing for a share of the existing economic resources to run our lives, than in discovering and inventing new ones because of the erroneous belief that luck is less sympathetic to more risk.

It is rational to fear luck. Only ignorance and arrogance can claim that any success or failure has nothing to do with Lady Luck. Sophisticated technological entrepreneurship is more dependent on sheer luck. Random theory rules the outcomes of ten business plans of any venture. Innumerable variables decide which one of the choices of the most calculating venture capitalist may cough up any return. In fact, most planning is about giving luck a measure. We may have patents, management team, great logic, marketing plan, and the cream of the best brains, but if luck is missing, we get swept into a drain. Scientific serendipity is really another name of luck. All superstitions have random luck as their origins. We can battle and beat up luck to some extent. Work, perseverance, optimism, keeping wide awake all the time gave us vulcanized rubber, light bulb, amplifier, microwave, lithium, copy machine and a host of other good things of life.

The world is full of infinite good luck and also bad luck. If everyone around us is lucky, we might get luckier if we are willing to continue and never stop working for it.

SHADOWY SMILES

The moment we are born, our minds are like highly absorptive but completely empty sponges; all our senses suck up without any discernment anything that comes their way, and a slurry and slush of stories and memories keeps building to saturate the innocent sponges. By the time our bodies cross the most formative, the first decade of life, most of us are cast like a bronze sculpture that has to be chiseled later to make any alterations. Along with all that is retained in our minds during our childhood, the patterns of our behavior and mental attitude toward the world are firmly ingrained. Precisely, the very tones of our speech with any associated rudeness, politeness, and gestures become part of our vocal cords and furrows on our foreheads. We never recognize the difference that the tones of our speech make on our wide and deep future; and how our smiles become shadowy.

We are born in an ocean of very powerful social, religious, cultural, racial, and political currents and depths. Rarely could one stand outside these currents and feel how the forces of these currents sway big masses of people into all kinds of constructive or destructive directions. We read, study, and assimilate history, human nature, philosophy, sociology, and a host of many related facts and still keep going through many cycles of rise and fall. As long as Providence does not decide to change human nature, we are destined to repeat the same fate many million times over. We may claim that a human is the finest, most gifted, and intelligent creature of nature, but she is also the only cursed one, for she is the only one who must collect and hoard more than is needed, eat more than the body is willing to accept, and, worst of all, enslave and kill her own kind for no good reason. And her will to conquer and rule her fellow beings comes alive at birth and dies with her death.

SPEED OF SMILE

The ends of our mental plans have never changed and shall never change. We have never stopped making progress and it has always been to satisfy the same old needs and more new wants but with new tools of technology. Progress has summarily meant faster fulfillment of our desires that have no finish line. Only the crawling evolution can change what the whole humanity has been going for forever – eliminating the uncertainty of tomorrow.

The most accepted measure of progress is the speed at which we run our lives. The faster we go, the more progressive we are. It is not only the speed of our physical body that is the measure of progress, but also the speed at which our minds race. Progress has no doubt brought many good things to life, but it does have many undesirable aspects too.

Beautiful landscapes have been littered with highways and byways to drag a one hundred and fifty pound body just for a few hours a day in a five thousand pound structure of glass and steel firing and fuming along the way. In most of the places where people concentrate and congregate, we see all the streets and roads lined up with eighteen-foot long monstrous vehicles occupied by three-foot wide bodies. How many more souls are now condemned to spend at least one fourth of their disposable time every day in addition to torturing their minds with stress to commute to make a living just because the speed has afforded them to live far and far away from their place of work! The speed is well known for killing in many different ways; it is also superb in saving the injured by racing them to hospitals and in allowing the criminals disappear in a spur of the moment.

Advancements in medical technology have to be commended for eradicating many dreadful diseases, increasing our life span, transplanting intricate organs, and diagnosing and treating deeply buried dangers. But it has also managed to build and fill up all the hospitals purely for the greed of medical professionals by imprisoning and keeping alive the very old in pain and misery until they slowly crawl to death.

Entertainment, fun, pleasures, and simple celebration of joy have been adulterated, complexed, and hijacked by the speed and sophistication of technology. Progress emphasizes that any joy without a cost is not worth having. Entertainment must be micro-planned, scheduled by the minute by professionals; our minds are no longer considered fit to plan our own relaxation and fun.

The foundation of progress, as we clearly see, is to plunder the earth as fast as possible, invent new needs and wants, design, produce and sell more products, build bigger homes to stuff them with more stuff, and to make sure that inhabitants do not use their homes for any purpose other than sleeping at night, and work twelve hours a day to make mortgage and debt payments and let the smile of life go to hell.

We are fortunate to be left with any disposable money after satisfying all our needs and unfortunate if we have to deal with any monotonous time. The mind is never still and is ever busy planning, even when its body is not willing to execute anything. It may not remember its own activities right after it wakes up from a deep slumber. It does not retain what it might have gone through during coma, under anesthesia, or very low blood pressure. But when it is up, it is the source of all problems, solutions, vices, and virtues. A mugger, a thug, a rescuer, a liberator, a sage, and a scammer - all are the products of its motion and commotion. What is the difference in the state of a mind that is in the process of mugging and a religious mind that is singing in praise of its creator, the God? These two minds cannot peer into each other and look at the tranquility of one and turbulences of the other.

The most blissful ignorance, if it is at all some kind of ignorance, is to feel that the universe has a sovereign and She is watching all our deeds; this is the only way all monsters will turn into angels and the heaven will descend to the earth for us to live a life of smiles.

We live and survive cocooned in a shell of ego as a part of our biological evolution. It is very difficult to crack out through the walls of this shell and become humble. Any kind of love for anyone or any goal makes our ego flexible but only for the selfish purpose of controlling or possessing the thing or the person; evidently, it is a tragic fact of life. As we go through the ups and downs of our lives, only a few of us realize that being genuinely respectful of others, i.e., being humble, has many rewards in terms of peace, happiness, and a smiling life.

Smile is a gesture. Communication of thought began with gestures; speech followed much later. Even today strong emotions are exhibited with strong gestures and words. No speech can be made forceful without appropriate gestures. Smile is the sweetest of all gestures and it is needed as a spice to make any communication by words tasteful and classy.

Smile does not go with any judicial deliberation. A judge smiling from the bench will be declared highly prejudicial; a judge has to learn how to appear grave in the most frivolous, hilarious or fraudulent presentations. Court room is one place where smile is dangerous. Any witness carrying a smile will be considered a liar. All questions, all statements, all depositions, all responses have to proceed with an air of true or fake emotionless expression. A law-professional dealing in lawlessness or lawfulness must wear a smile-less expression to render a well considered and unbiased opinion.

FROM GOD HERSELF!

From lowly to lofty living entities
Be proud for you are not the lowest
Did I fail in making you upright?
The question is irrelevant
For My creation is forever transient

I'm so amused and entertained
To notice that you humans are so assured
Of many observations that you made
To proclaim that you have discovered
The perpetual laws of your God
You merely witness through your flawed perception
You believe infallible conclusions
Conclusions that are truly illusions

Remember!
Nothing in My universe is perpetual
I love transformation,
Expansion and contraction
So, it is the change that is eternal

What an evil act of execution
Of intoxicating your essence
Particularly in My image and name
You annihilate much of your own kind
By proclaiming to be My messengers
To keep on massacring non-believers

You were never born
And nor shall you ever die
I have embedded perpetual life
Into every cell of yours.
Next to creating TIME
Implanting life into so minute a space
Was the most difficult task of Me.

All souls are dispatched to earth barehanded
And are ordained to return barehanded
They leave with smiles when dispatched
Alas, they all return desponded
May be they are unhappy about becoming bald-headed
Or more truly late in life very feebleminded
I must alter humans before their journey is concluded
So they all return to Me simpleminded and smiled

DECORATIONS OF THE FACE

What we wear on our faces every moment and every day impacts our hearts and minds and also of those we interact with, more than any other decoration on our face. We are talking here not of material matter but of the expressions we wear. We may have exotic ornaments on our ears, noses, tongues, chins and eye brows, necklaces on our necks, rainbow hairpieces or caps on our head to turn some heads our way; but how our faces dart and gaze can create hells and heavens in our lives.

Face is the most conspicuous organ of our body and also of our soul. It speaks of us and for us even when we do not speak a word. Its wrinkles and crinkles reveal where we have been and are going to. The facial expressions that accompany the tones of our speech can attribute radically diverse meanings to exactly the same words.

So, dress your face with a simple sincere smile. It will carry you to many pleasant places you have never been to. It may build you the fortune you have been dreaming of. It will earn you the most prized reward called peace of mind at no expense. It will keep your heart beating a lot longer. Most briefly it will let you live a heavenly life right on this planet.

FREEDOM
TO SMILE IN CHAINS

Historians perhaps have an easy job doing their jobs; it is to tell true stories in simple words. But their allegiance to certain race, country, religion, or region makes them use different verbs and adjectives for the same acts of aggression and invasion. All invaders sought fame and power through massacres, plunder, destruction, and human misery. But to historians, some invaders were warriors, some barbarians, some great, some heroes, some monsters, some tyrants, some conquerors, and some great robbers. Alexandra was The Great, Napoleon a Liberator, Chinghis Khan not So Great, Ashoka only a King, Stalin nearly A Monster, and Hitler a Real Monster.

The art of economics is another product of human biased and misleading thinking. It is supposed to deal with most efficient use of scarce tangible and intangible resources. It also gives birth to analysts who claim to know where we should invest our savings to multiply more than if a bum randomly invested them. In the long run, we all find that the bums were no bummer than the sophisticated analysts. The seed and tree of all economic progress is the invisible hand of self-interest. This invisible hand is maimed, crippled, cut off, and mutilated by ever increasing licenses, permits, and regulations invented by politicians. Further, all the great theories of great economists are crippled. Besides, the economists have invented many mathematical formulations with all kinds of variables to interlink various economic resources, without ever including the most important variable and ingredient called political toxicity. Maybe for this reason we see: all the intelligence and analysis of all the economists of all times put together cannot predict, even to some close approximation, what the next day, next month or next year is going to bring to us in terms of economic boom or bust. We must learn to smile in the chains of freedom that is so criminally provided by morons's powered politicians.

Smile was ordained by nature to take a seat on lips; simplicity was ordained to be smile's subordinate. Alas, then education and learning took hold of intelligence and men invented technology and philosophy. Soon from nature's fields popped up humongous metropolises. Men also acquired wisdom, penned millions of books, uncovered many secrets of God and arrived at the sophisticated conclusion that smile can never go with any truthful deduction and solemn speech. Sedateness became rule of life that progressed into complexity from simplicity. Men rationalized why to annihilate each other in the name of justice. Smile got lost in the realm of brilliance.

HUMANS SMILEIZED

How do humans transport, convey, live, make or fail their lives to finally return to their heavenly destination? And how do their livelihood styles fold into their faces and minds?

From the best to the worst in terms of achievements, impact on humanity, peace, love and comfort, they can be rated from 1- the best to 10-the worst.

1.Geniuses: –They are totally lost in unfolding the secrets of God. Money and fame, they care not for. Born once in a century, or one in a billion men, they change the directions of humanity. Only the greatest of physicists and mathematicians make this category. A few of them are: Newton, Maxwell, Einstein, Fermat, Euler, Lagrange, and Gauss. They come with the most unpretentious, humble and peaceful souls. They are born with serene inner smiles.

2. Discoverers and inventors, academic theorists: – They are the scientists in top academic schools and research institutes that expand the work of geniuses in many directions. Money and fame is of little temptation to them.

3. Wealth creators – They apply proven technology and information to generate wealth and employment of an amazing order. They should be credited for smiles of the world.

4. Entertainers, poets, musicians, playwrights – They portray and play life's joys, tragedies, emotions, laughter, good and bad times to let days and years roll by softly. Without them many will perish of boredom.

5. God's messengers–They invent all kinds of Gods and Goddesses to direct and send their followers to hell or heaven. To be taken genuine they have to look serious all their lives; they keep their smile less faces painted with fake Godly power.

6. Executives – They work for the wealth creators in many roles, and have little vision of their own. Their smiles are as planned as their work plans.

7. Small entrepreneurs – They grow to be moderately rich and get stuck with their routine never to breathe freely. Trying hard to become big they fail due to lack of good vision. They find that freedom is not free, just as a smile is too.

8. Human-robots, slaves and servants – They totally lack original thinking. Almost 95% population falls in this category. They love to take orders and hate to think for themselves. Academic degrees do not free them from this slavery. Like mechanized components of a machine, their brains get programmed when to smile and when not to.

9. Morons –criminals, alcoholics, drug addicts and public (government) employees. Their minds are petrified; they cannot feel or sense the meaning of a smile.

10. Monarchs and politicians make this category that stands at the lowest rung of human ladder. Their main objective is to rob and curb human-freedom. They use vicious means to capture and hold on to power for their nefarious ends, and are evil incarnated. Freedom and sincere smile are unintelligible concepts to them.

SMILE OF ENNUI

Here is a little true philosophy of life we live by that robs us of real smiling happiness.

Once in a while, on a fine peaceful morning, in bright sunshine, under the shadow of a majestic tree, by a stream, lake or river, we should sit down alone to contemplate how the control mechanism of our lives is working. To put our thinking on a clean and clear background we have to be in an open vast huge blue sky. Enclosed in an artificial setting we cannot look at ourselves due to many distractions. A little thinking in a great natural enclosure may show us that we are not in control of ourselves but under the control of all kinds of weird stuff; and that we are so tranced, programmed and brainwashed that our lives are direction less and messy.

Let us examine a typical day of a typical one of us. We cannot lump together the whole world population. Fundamentally, there is not that much of a difference between the routines of the rich and the poor, high techs and low techs, Americans and Chinese, mind workers and physical workers, employees and self- employed. Close to two-thirds of each day is spent sleeping, eating, a little socializing, and commuting to and from the place of work; the remaining one-third of each day is consumed in actual livelihood. Save for a tiny fraction of the whole humanity that is engaged in discovering and inventing; the rest of us are busy cloning one thing or the other within some configuration of a few walls and a ceiling all our lives. At the end of each day of cloning, the needs of our bodies and minds are more or less alike. Boredom is the most prevalent outcome of all the routine we go through year after year for at least two-thirds of our lives.

Boredom is the seed of drug business, universal consumption of alcohol, gambling, wasteful entertainment industry, juvenile destructive behavior, many kinds of crimes, and in the American scene even the cause of shooting and killing rampage in schools.

The lack of real interest in our natural surroundings, our own family and friends, unfounded worries about tomorrow, and some constructive hobbies result in boredom, loneliness and a state of mind medically termed depression. Peaceful social, cultural, and familial interactions are the best drugs to treat depression; our advancement and preoccupation with the good things of life are robbing us of these free remedies.

When all our basic needs are satisfied, our wants take their turn to sprout endlessly and expand faster than the means available to quench them. The less effort it takes to fulfill needs and wants, the more expensive is the treatment of boredom. Just as no pharmaceutical company tries to discover any drug to cure any disease but only to continually treat it, all industry and business to ward off boredom only breed addiction to their products with no lasting benefit. Hard drugs, like cocaine and heroin, mercilessly decay minds; soft drugs, like alcohol do that mercifully; squatting before a slot machine, a human acting like a machine pulling a lever up and down a million times is a sign of an empty mind waiting to brim up with coins. The entertainment industry is in the business of obscuring boredom, not in treating or curing it.

With proper planning and brainwashing any kind of service or goods can be unloaded to anyone. The sales skill lies in creating customers who neither need nor can afford to pay for what they are sold. The fun industry does an excellent job of convincing us that fun is located at least one thousand miles away from where we live, and only the marketing experts know how to ward off our boredom by minute-to-minute micro planning for us and by telling us that we need to lock ourselves into their gigantic vessels, resorts and hotels in order to experience real relaxation, and that we must gorge on an immense amount of edible stuff to enjoy life. We are told that without plundering the Mother Earth, no fun is complete and a smile possible.

SMILE- THE BOTTOM LINE

We have bases within and without us that determine the peace we enjoy or the turmoil we suffer from. The familial, religious, cultural, and social environment we were raised in forms the frame of our minds for our inner peace. The politicians of our own and neighboring countries decide how much peace they will let us live in; historically, politicians and peace have rarely coexisted. Of the two sides of human nature, the ghastly side is far bigger than the pleasant side.

Due to man's mostly dreadful innate nature, planning for, securing, and maintaining peace have consumed the largest portion of expensive resources all through the history and all over the globe. Men, individually and in groups, never ceased to attack their next-door and far off neighbors for economic, religious, racial, and many other prejudicial reasons.

The most heinous and ugly part of human nature shows up in crimes committed against the very weak and helpless; kidnapping children, abusing the elderly, murdering infants, and assaulting dependent women are commonly practiced terrors in rich and poor countries alike.

The fences we build, the guns we carry, the security systems we employ, the locks we install, the safe deposit boxes we rent, and the police we need are all the means needed to save ourselves from the nefarious activities of our fellow humans living right in our own neighborhood. The army, navy, air force and the weaponry to annihilate all the life from the face of the globe have been created to save the rulers from their far off neighbors. All military powers are truly for the rulers of one country to save themselves from the rulers of other country. Working people of the world are too busy in their own livelihood and simultaneously feeding the rulers to hate or attack anyone. The Russians, the Americans, the Chinese, and the Vietnamese basically want to coexist in peace, but the rulers of all these people spend large resources to build walls of hatred among them.

In comparison with the bad side, the good side of human nature is miniscule. For every one godly Mother Teresa who gave her life for love and peace, a thousand monstrous Alexanders, Napoleans, Hitlers, and Stalins come to the world to plunder, massacre, and enslave; many such monsters are very much in power today and are the cause of misery and poverty of at least three-fourths of the humanity in various parts of the world. We should define a monster as the one who simply to satisfy his own hunger of power controls the freedom of others by inflicting all kinds of atrocities. No act is more criminal than not letting the born-free live free and die-free.

Yes, we all are very kind, loving and helpful to our own close blood relatives, parents, children, grandchildren, etc. Yet this does not speak for any good side of human nature. How we treat those who are financially or emotionally dependent on us as employees, spouses, or otherwise, or are easily replaceable, or have no blood or physical relationship with us, determines our true nature. In contrast to the foregoing, how we treat those on whom we are financially and emotionally dependent, and who are irreplaceable, and who have no physical or blood relationship with us does not show our inner self. In this situation, we are courteous, respectful, orderly, organized, and disguised to the utmost degree of goodness.

The primary difference between wisdom and stupidity is the ability to guess the long- term and, at large scale, the consequences of our deeds. Our nature has intimate relationships with these two opposite poles of our future. The fastest way to enjoy a ton of money is to rob a bank, and spending all the loot before getting caught; the slowest way is to acquire immense amounts of knowledge, make a great invention, monopolize its application, and enjoy it at leisure without ever worrying about getting caught. We can look into many phases of our lives and can easily decide whether our nature is leading us into stupidity or wisdom

Human nature in disguise is normally pleasant, in naked form ugly. We change our tones, salutations, gestures, physical presentation and response time to exhibit our nature in disguise. We can look authoritative or slavish, kind or cruel, attractive or ugly, friendly or indifferent without much effort; it all depends on whether we are on the receiving or giving end at the moment.

GOD'S SMILE
AFTER MAN

God came into being very mysteriously
All by Her own unbounded authority
There is no beginning or end to Her creativity
She is also beyond the law of causality
To think, that She had to be created, is absurdity
Let us all simply get lost in Her Infinite Majesty
This is all that goes into eternity

She has been a SHE by Her Own perpetuity
By Her plan, only a female may hold all the vitality

After God came into existence
She conceived and created the universe
All the stars, planets, black holes and galaxies
Visible and invisible materials
Gravitation, light, electrons, neutrons and positrons
Trees, plants, shrubs, creepers, flowers and fruits
Rivers, stream, oceans and mountains
She paid particular attention to planet earth
No reason is known, why?

Then God was lost and faced a serious question

She saw no one to appreciate and enjoy Her
creation
Was this all She had done in vain!

She ordered a conference with all Her lieutenants
And declared, She didn't see any use of Her
creations
For, no one was there to appreciate Her
innovations
Her lieutenants pondered with their big brains
And came up with an invention with simple
wittiness

Man was the invention, of their best
imaginations

So, this is how man came into life
All happy and smiling all the time
God gave him joy and immortality
She was very proud of Her ingenuity
To watch man enjoying Her grandiosity

But soon, She was envious of man's joy
She saw him super pure happy with no worries
He was singing, dancing, enjoying like eternally
Running the universe had become stressful to God
She summoned her deputies to help out again
Her man should not be so happy and worry-less

Deputies easily crafted someone to woo God's
man
And they named the new creation a woo-man
The woo-man was in God's own vision
God designed woo-man to seize man's totality
After God placed woo-man into man's reality
Never shall man now see freedom of his mentality

Man has devised infinite techniques
To invent, craft and produce objects
Ear rings, nose rings, and tongue rings
Castles, gardens, rugs, beds and carriages
Exquisite Colognes, diamonds and gems
And writes love-poems, romance songs and plays
To please, satisfy and gratify God's lively creation
And abbreviated the name woo-man to woman

Woman can now adorn her body by the million
All men now suffer from serious disorientation
For they are now ceaselessly in intoxication
Woman is now man's everlasting occupation
God is very happy in woman's perpetuation
And woman is happier in man's commotion
Women, therefore, smile a lot more than men

SMILE
FOR SURVIVAL

People of many ancient civilizations have left for us a great inheritance in the form of inscription of their experiences with life. They did not have the means for instantaneous gratification of their needs and wants. Their minds and muscles had been busier inventing and discovering than are ours, because they had to fight the elements at a closer range just to keep alive. In relative terms, the improvements they made in each generation were not insignificant. They were scattered in small and large groups all over the globe with little or no communication; that is why many languages and cultures took birth and grew. Not many of these groups enjoyed peaceful life; they invaded, attacked, massacred, and enslaved each other frequently just for being richer, weaker, not worshipping the same god, having skin of different color, or not speaking the same language.

Some of these ancient groups were perhaps strong enough to defend themselves for centuries and were able to build lasting religious cultures that are not only alive today, but are gaining belief and strength all over the world. The latest medical research has supported the health benefits claimed by those ancient discoveries. Some of these discoveries were only about the links between the state of mind and physical health. Modern medicine followed suit only recently, realizing that the relationship between our ailments and our thoughts are very strong.

Nature has gifted us with fight or flight instinct for survival with a smile, so we do not know, when and how the concept of peace came about and to which ancient civilization the origin of this concept should be credited. We do know that the power hungry, the invaders, the warriors, and the wantons do not and did not dream of it. Peace is these entire ingredients compounded: tranquility, serenity, freedom from anxiety, feeling of security, lack of mental agitation, selfless and harmless attachment with something or someone, and above all, hatred for none.

Smile is an essential prescription for surviving under stress. Stress is an upshot of taking life too gravely and broodingly. At the same time, stress is a necessary evil; without it one would die of boredom. Though all repetitive work is stressful and monotonous, it too is a necessary evil; it fatigues body and brain for a good night sleep. What dances under the skull dictates very appreciably much that happens to every organ of the body; let that dance smile as much as it can to heal and restore the mind to its natural nobility.

GOODNESS AND SMILE WITHOUT GOD!

The most momentous problem logicians face is how humans can be persuaded to become virtuous without fear of the supernatural of any form. A truly virtuous society under any system of faiths has never existed and shall never survive. The faiths and religions are the inventions of our minds; and our minds cannot devise any pure virtue subordinate to any concept. We shall, therefore, forever be at the mercy of fanaticism and programming of the mind.

Real smile is not possible without peace. Peace is not possible without an imaginary God. Imaginary God is not possible without imagination. Imagination is not possible without a blind mind. A blind mind is the biggest source of happiness. But blind mind has its own dangerous blinders. Smile can be made a trait of mind irrationally. And that is true fortunately.

HUNTING FOR A HAPPY SMILE

Happiness, an imaginary possession, is only a state of mind that has little to do with material goods.

Pursuit of happiness is the bottom line at the end of every day, every month, every year, and also at the close of the life itself. It has also been claimed to be an inalienable right in the Declaration of Independence. Each one of us is constantly busy like a bee, either doing a lot or a little to attain to this illusive state of mind. A state of mind it only is, for no one could ever establish that it has any relationship with any external possessions or lack thereof. Gather all that has been written, talked, discussed, theorized on this abstract object, and we shall have more volumes of paper than the rest of the information combined. Since antiquity, all religious leaders have prayed to help their followers acquire all kind of means for the end called happiness. No recipe, technology, pill, or concoction has been discovered to manufacture the most wanted thing of all times.

The entity called happiness is in unlimited supply and is free, but it is always at top of the list of the least possessed items. It is most sought after, but astonishingly least acquired, possessed, and visible. The true reason of this strange phenomenon appears to be the possibility that the mind is not evolved or designed to stay in a relaxation mode. Therefore smiling facial expressions are not generally common.

DIVINE SMILE

Is the origin of life and species a random 'survival of the fittest' process, or is there something divine about it? Why don't evolutionists claim that the beginning, changes, contraction, and expansion of the universe are also some kind of evolutionary processes? The real meaning of evolution has never been clearly explained and agreed to. The latest revelations on the intricate structure of the DNA that stores all the codes of conception, formation, growth, aging, multiplication and end of life, along with repair and healing of all the physiological and anatomical systems when diseased or accidentally damaged, above all the mysterious consciousness that is really the real life, should cast serious doubts on the theory of evolution. It is very hard to accept, that any random process, even in a span of a trillion years, could have arranged all the components of the DNA so sequentially and logically in order to perpetuate and multiply life for an infinite time in a precise and well-ordered scheme. DNA stores all the genetic information of a whole life, from conception to death, and all the lives that follow it forever and ever. Three billion nucleotide pairs make up the genetic code of a normal human cell, and over one billion amino acids can be characterized by the genetic code; from the possible one billion amino acids, our body chooses only about twenty combinations to structure and function itself. The theory of evolution is too simplistic, naïve, and raw and should not carry much weight if we consider the mystical processes that convert the information contained in DNA into a life that is conscious and has a mind. God can tell us now that not only the heavens are infinite; the molecular intricacies of every point of life are also infinite.

The theory of evolution is believable if it is considered attached to some sort of pre planned divine blue print, for then it could be called a divine evolution that is what it appears to be. If consciousness is what life really is, and if the brain is its only abode, then the size of the physical body that houses, feeds and protects the consciousness, must have some meaningful proportional size relationship to it. Human body size is either too big or too small for the size of the brain it has to feed, protect, and carry around. It is too big, because a one foot tall body could have easily met all the nourishment and achievement needs of the brain; also, Mother Nature would have been much less devastated by a one foot tall animal.

All actions, emotions, expressions, thoughts, birth, death, and all else there is, is perpetually built into a kind of inexplicable infinite divinity. Keep on smiling for 'know thyself' is an irrelevant idiom.

God Almighty! Don't Smile

Men have exercised all the might of their minds to impose the words of their prophets on all who refused to accept their extremism. They traveled far and wide with their swords and guns. Blood of infidels is to them devotion to their God. Massacre binges have been spiritual entertainment to them. Their God has reserved for them heavenly abode next to His own throne. Sacrificing their own life on the name of their God is the greatest victory for them. How deeply can mind be tranced!

Of all walls dividing mankind at all times and all places, the walls built in the name of Gods have endured longest and strongest. These walls have caused more torment, bloodshed and hatred than walls of money, race and language. No knowledge of any kind in any amount alters the mind that is saturated with a certain kind of God from the very childhood. The Real God cannot have any semblance with any of many Gods that human mind has invented. The Real God cannot be conceptualized, given any form or characterized; SHE cannot have special affinity for humankind. Somehow, mind has been blessed or cursed to liberate or enslave itself in numerous ways.

Smile to be effective may or may not need an attractive set of teeth lined up behind a set of slender or lumpy lips. Many a time a smile radiating through very crooked set of teeth is very pleasing. Orthodontists all over the world have misused and overused smile as a marketing tool to fatten up their pockets. Again, a smile beaming from eyes is less fake and more sincere than the one turning out from lips. The people, on whom orthodontists have performed their skills, tend to smile more to exhibit the big investment they have made in their mouths. No doubt a beautiful set of teeth does decorate any face and is an asset in some ways.

SMILE
OF LIVELIHOOD

To understand how best we can produce good things of life efficiently and without aggravation is a difficult task. Adam Smith, a social philosopher and economist born about three hundred years ago, was a genius of a kind; he understood and explained how to integrate human nature and nature's nature to create wealth. He could see that each one of us is only interested in oneself and would do anything good or evil to increase one's own short- or long-term economic security and gain depending upon each individual's intelligence and stupidity. He named this perpetual self-interest 'the invisible hand'. The difficult part of this simple and easy to understand principle is how to implement it. The politicians, and the executors of their rules and orders - the bureaucrats, generally being of lowest intelligence, try to maximize the return of their paper work and red tapes on a short-time basis. The invisible hand works for them within the limits of their stupidity. The rest of the population is led by the invisible hand only within the limits allowed by boorish politicians and bureaucrats. The wealth or poverty of nations is, therefore, most significantly determined by insanity and poverty of the minds of the politicians in power. The fact that most of the world most of the time has suffered from poverty speaks of imbecility of its rulers.

Preparing for a livelihood to stay alive and healthy is the primary skill one must learn. Teaching this skill well and efficiently is the most difficult skill. All livelihoods are forms of trading with one element in common: fetching more than shelling out. Creating, mass-producing, and selling tangible products are as old as human history. Changing civilization has given us novel methods of livelihood; all kinds of mental skills full of many varieties of knowledge and information can be traded. This method has one unique advantage: the inventory does not occupy any physical space and the useful stock increases as it is exhausted. Also, certified and licensed bodies can consume the consumer by due process of law as long as they want to by creating more rules, procedures, and ambiguous laws. The diversity of services and materials traded for livelihood are only limited by human ingenuity that knows no bounds.

The tragedy associated with most skills for making a living is the boredom and sickening stress that descends on our lives due to repetitive and non-challenging nature of the responsibilities we have to carry out. As time goes by, even the work that we loved to begin with and clamored for smolders our hearts and minds. This is the reason why the quitting time of every day and weekends, holidays, and vacations are anxiously waited for. Most, who work for others, if given choice between going and not going to work and still getting paid, will choose abstaining. They want to have fun, take it easy, and live a life.

The task of making a living, if not enjoyable, is burdensome and also causes many health problems. For those who work for themselves, even repetitive dull work is not so dull, because they receive superior return of their hard work. Livelihood must be a joy for the life to be enjoyable. No life could be superior to the one that is in love with the process of earning a living with a smile.

PESSIMISTIC SMILE

My mind is scarred beyond repair
And my body is invisibly withered
I don't see any future in my future
My present crawls and it hurts
As my present rolls into the past
I sit to ponder the futility of life

This is Kinku's existence speaking
Kinku is an orphan,
Born in a poverty-stricken Indonesian village
Kinku has vivid memory of all the sufferings
The meaning of the words mom and dad
And of a friend too
He cannot comprehend
He does not feel or see being needed by anyone
He thinks,
Life is only about a little food and shelter

Kinku muses like a philosopher,
The past cannot be undone
One cannot see beyond the present
The present is omnipotent
Past teaches little or not at all
A lot is wanted though little is needed
One struggles against struggles most of the life

Is there really anything to be happy about!
Or, to be unhappy about!
Kinku wears a gloomy smile and believes
The answer is 'No'

SMILE
OF SIMPLICITY

Simplicity needs
Few tools
Not many theories and words
Only a little direction
To reach the destination.

Let affairs not be affairs
But simple fairs of pleasures
Simplicity listens more and speaks less
It is the shortest route to success

Truth resides in the beauty of simplicity
To strip off superfluity to come to
vivacity
Nature rules through absolute efficiency
For it rules out all complexity

Simplicity is not materialistic
But purely and truly spiritualistic
Walk the path of simplicity
If you are sure of your audacity

To ward off any kind of scarcity
Live a life of simplicity
If you want to talk of authenticity
Go with love, hope and tranquility

Let your tongue be simple and sweet
If you want to treat all without a treat

Smile goes stress-free with simplicity
With it a smile begets ecstasy
To smile with supreme superiority
Simply let it radiate with modesty

FOUNDATION OF SMILES

Family is a relatively simple and peaceful affair when both mother and father are biological parents of the kids living with them. When a stepmother, a stepfather, or stepchildren become part of the same household, life of the children is mostly emotionally disturbed and their mental growth stunted. A child who has to live with a stepparent is unfortunate. Statistics, true stories, and myths all confirm the same fact of the step parenthood; a rich child is poor when she does not have her own biological parents to take care of her. Sociologists confirm that only a small fraction of stepparents have any real feeling for their stepchildren.

The economic and sexual freedom in progressive cultures has one great tragic consequence, viz., continually accelerating divorce rate. The long-term bottom line of most divorces is disastrous to children and society, but nothing this fact would teach; many facets of humanity are ill, and divorce is only one of those ills. In the smoke of passion and narrow self-interest, nothing good appears visible. All the technological sophistication of the child day care centers, the theories of child psychologists, and the latest intelligence sharpening gadgets cannot replace the simple, primitive, instinctive love and care that even an illiterate parent provides a child for her superb growth.

It is the lack of real natural love that is responsible for sprouting criminal, idle, and ambition-less minds; we wander into wilderness when we employ all the geniuses to figure out why a child goes on shooting rampage in her school. Wealth beyond a certain point is perilous to the health of any family, because it increases the distance between parents and children both physically and mentally. It is also a cause of interference in the family atmosphere because it brings in outsiders in the form of servants, nannies, and maids. Results are so obvious, for most of the great and successful people are the product of middle class families; wealth, particularly inherited wealth, has rarely created great minds. Ills of a family, a society and a country take birth in the family unit and then grow and spread like cancer everywhere else. Family is the foundation of our smiles and this fact shall not change until the evolution process alters our brain chemistry.

PURSUIT OF SILENT SMILE

God may be a discovery, an invention, a fanciful fictional imagination, a peculiar source of entertainment, a wall to lean against, or whatever. Wrong or right, those who believe in Her are fortunate. They can find some purpose of life and go for it with joy and contentment, and that can give them a feeling of accomplishment. Their minds are more relaxed. Their disposable time and money are less destructive. This ignorance of believing in God, if at all it is ignorance, is bliss for them. And they should smile over it.

To run our minds in this seriously flawed real or unreal world, both science and religion or God is indispensable. Balance between the two is difficult to grasp. Science tells of the material facts for physical comforts, and religion helps us make distinction between good and evil for comfort of the mind. Unfortunately, religion distorts our thinking a lot more than science does. Religion is also a kind of drug that our rulers can intoxicate us with to sacrifice our lives against those who want to replace them. The religious leaders have caused a lot more bloodshed than scientists have. Getting fooled by the sentinels of God is the primary danger we face due to believing in Her. This fact has robbed mankind of peace and smiling existence.

THAT SUFFICES!

Smile may yield ecstasy, or it could be in the reverse order. Either way, smile is the mantra of all mantras for the body and mind to dance in the order that nature has devised to last the life for the longest time with least number of pains.

Smile provides with the path and latitude in many ordinary facets of daily life. A little of it lets others yield the road for you. A little of it gets the help you may need. A little of it wins you a better bargain. A little of it may let you receive the order you are looking for. A little of it may put you on top of the hill or heap of success. A little of it may find you the most likable person in a crowd of many. A little of it may demand that you be the leader. A little of it may find you in your mirror always smiling.

SMILE
A GLOBAL ENTERPRISE

The yellow man, the white man
The black man and the red man
And truly everywhere everyman

Man of any culture and civilization
And of any society and sophistication
Without any kind of discrimination

Man may speak French or English
German, Italian or Spanish
Chinese, Japanese or Polish
Or may be totally outlandish

To buy or sell
Wheel or deal
Win or prevail
Bargain or haggle

To argue assertively
Articulate authoritatively
Communicate conclusively
Learn comprehensively
Listen pensively
Love expressively
Pray meditatively
Speak seductively
Stroll decoratively
Teach perceptively

One must learn
How to smile
When to smile
For whom to smile
How much to smile
These are the elements of smile
Of a global enterprise

Smile is the most important ingredient, element and secret for flirting. You must let your glances dance, open your postures, move your eyebrows around, run your fingers through your hair, ask stupid questions, dart your eyes and roll your head meaninglessly, all with a smile to be effective.

Smile is psychotherapy, physiotherapy and therapy of all therapies to heal the wounds of all wrongs that occurred or might occur. It drives down blood pressure, sinks stress, enhances immune system and improves efficiency of all physiological commands.

'Smile', yes, it can be faked, frilled, forged or feigned. All this fakery can't be hidden. Smile of the eyes is an integral part of any unreserved smile. All components of our body can lie, but eyes can't. So, let there be a sincere and simple smile for the life to sail smoothly.

LET THE HEART SMILE
SERENELY

Except for a few upheavals now and then, like earthquakes, tornadoes, and floods, the working of Mother Nature is peaceful and pleasant. Sun rises and sets, little seeds become towering trees, flowers bloom by the trillions, tigers dash at high speed, billions of gallons of water rises off the ocean floor, hearts keep beating, lungs breathing, kidneys cleansing, all noiselessly and disturbing nothing beyond their own realms. It is a kind of philosophical noninterference and hidden wisdom of all natural phenomena. We have an important lesson to learn from this observation: Concentration on our own good goals can do us a great good.

SMILE OF THE SOUL

You must realize
You are awfully fragile
If only for a little while
Your brain property
Is devoid of blood supply
Your mind shall yelp good bye
Your body may not die
Heart may keep on beating
Lungs may stay breathing
Liver may go on working
Kidneys may continue cleaning
But the brain shall cease sensing
You shall be vegetating
And permanently relaxing
To heaven or hell you shall be travelling
No telling where to you shall be reaching

Sooner or later
One way or the other
You shall be on for departure
Despite, you came from wherever
So, be humble, never brash
For you can perish in a flash
Why take any bitterness
With your soul
Into perpetual nothingness

Don't be arrogant and vile
While you are free and alive
Live and let others live
Smile and let others smile

Smile
Comes with human genes
absolutely

But has to be nurtured
from infancy

With the right culture
to keep it lively

A SMILE OF LIFE

Here is the question without an end
When and how this thing called mind
Enters into a mass of cells of any kind
To turn the completed living body
Into a wondrous working intellect

Body and mind wear
But not evenly ever
Sometimes when body resigns
And if mind too quits
You should celebrate in heavens
As soon as your soul arrives
But when mind surrenders
And vitality of body continues
The body alters into a machine
Simply to be fed and excrete

Remember, let life take a freeway
Laugh, sing, dance, read and pray
Dedicate, concentrate, meditate and portray
Talk, walk, link, love, think and defray
Don't agitate, stink, balk and stray
Smile, reflect, march, stroll and wander away
Into the path of peace of smile like a holiday

THE EVENTUAL ENIGMA

Curiosity is an important ingredient of an active and productive life. We spend dreadful amounts of time in many trifling ideas, incidents, and their consequences. Why don't we try to discover a little of ourselves! The biological functions of our body have been well researched and we can readily get molecular details of any part of it, but our thoughts and memories make what we are: we should be anxious to understand the beginning and the end of the thinking mechanisms, and all that goes in between the two. Not much is known for certain, but whatever has been identified is very fascinating.

THE SMILE OF EYES

The most beautiful and bountiful,
The most hopeful and helpful,
The most gorgeous and good-looking,
The most trustworthy and truthful,
The most friendly and faithful,
Is the smile of eyes.

All muscles are slaves of power of the mind.
But muscles can't control brightness of eyes.
Eyes speak of fortune and fate,
Of love, hatred, anger and agony
And surprise, suffering and misery
Eyes can be bright and glassy
Dull, attentive or smoky
Smiling with eyes is the mystery,
That can't be like a fakery

THE SMILE OF TIME

Scientists have delved into time
For its nature is truly sublime
Since it launched the universe
Its history may be brief or long
But its supremacy is forever strong
Philosophizing on time is hilarious
For it is the ultimate mystery of cosmos

How very omnipotent and omnipresent
Time is an entity that cannot be defined
No phenomenon as direction of time
Is comprehensible or explainable

Far more than God, the Almighty
The origin and cause of time is
More indefinable and mysterious
More strange and glorious
More elusive and multifarious

Unthinkable, strange, but true
Time shall cease to run
If transfer or form of energy stops
Time is the cause of change
And change is the cause of time

Past is lost forever, present does not stop
Future does not wait, no matter what you do
If day, night, life and ageing disappears
Direction of time will be incomprehensible
Ageing process makes us think
That time can only go forward

Time can be measured
Only by repetitive changes
If such changes did not occur
Time shall have no scale to measure with
How to measure time, does not define it

In time, we are born and live
And finally return to meet our maker
It is time that sickens and heals
Time empowers and makes luck lively
At times tragically and at times blissfully

Time and luck accompany ceaselessly
For both go hand-in-hand eternally
Some kill time, but time kills all

Fast and slow randomly, time flows
At times it crawls, at times soars
It is time that enriches and destitutes
Honor thy time, every moment of it
Be proud, if this is your habit

Smile with time, for time and in time
At good times and bad times
As much as you can anytime

SELLING BY A SMILE

Smile inarguably paves smoothly all paths of life. Selling and smile are close loving companions. But the execution of the project of intertwining smile with selling is far from easy. A smile can't be demanded, imposed or enforced. However, it can be taught in a very subtle educative process. The very minds of the disciples of the School of Smiles have to be focused into simple sincerity. Car dealers have totally failed in teaching car salespersons how to greet and smile at prospective car buyers. There are zillions of sales men, women, girl and boys, who all wait for the quitting time after lousy selling chores; they should be titled cashiers for they hardly do any selling. Politicians are the best imposters of all skills; their trade is how to convincingly lie with a smile. Those, who are slaves of monopolistic government bodies, don't need learning any pleasantries; they live and expire like robots; smiling at their wage-payers is incomprehensible to them.

Smile to a significant degree is an important product of monetary rewards. Money-power plays its power in all aspects of life. It generates all kinds of looks - good, bad and middle-of-the-road. Money-power is no less moral or immoral than rest of all the powers. In the matter of gestures of smile and laughter, money-power shows or hides its degree relative to what is around it; one on the highest rung always has the first and last word with or without a smile.

Smile has been the victim of many researchers. What is a researcher? It is a question with a million speculative answers. Psychologists are researchers that read into conduct and deeds of talking creatures, precisely humans; these intellectuals are programmed surrounded by very limited cultural avenues. Most of their exalted theories fall flat in the real life applications, so we see crime statistics at a standstill every where in the world. Often funny conclusions accomplish them than the other way round. One male psychologist deduced: (1) good-looking men become more friendly and handsome as they grow older than unattractive ones. (2) Gorgeous women become less beautiful and friendly as they grow older than ordinary ones. (3) More they smile, less real they seem. (4) Female smiles are less faithful than male smiles. (5) Female smile is like a 'business as usual', male smile is 'meaningful and authentic'. The foregoing deduction deduces the deduction that men are deducible to a dumber degree than the dumbest women.

SMILE OF WISDOM

From birth to death
Life needs breath
It must go on without pause
Whatever the cause

Life begins with nothing
Also ends with nothing
In between all that
It runs on blood and sweat

Three times every day
Every moment of existence
Food must go down the esophagus
Though only a little is needed daily
But it is stuffed in profusely

A roof over the head big or trivial
Is also basic for survival
The roof and all the glitters
Have no end to its limits

We keep on learning
How to continue earning
Vast sums of money
All through life's journey
With failure and success
We can't interrupt this process

Little of life is spared
For what should be cared
Love and compassion
Don't see any reason
To provide any satisfaction

Past never was, future never shall be
Whatever happens, is in the present
Whatever would happen tomorrow
Shall happen when tomorrow is today

What is reality and what illusion
Is the question no one can rejoin
From east, west, north and south
And all nooks of the earth

For many millennium
Saints, philosophers and scientists
Have failed to break the mystery of mind

The true path to freedom
And seeds of wisdom
Lie in laughter and smile
To make life purely versatile

Smile is an indication of a happy life! Is it really! Are smiling, frowning, screaming, shouting, yelling and all such styles of running a life actually cultural characteristics or neurobiological reaction to social freedom or dependence? Is it better to wear fake but pleasant face than real but unpleasant one? Life keeps on going dominated by the forces of culture and good and bad laws. There is little one can do to alter one's life style under these constraints.

Smile is born with the very birth of us all. You may be faithful, faithless or lacking in all faiths that you can imagine of, you can't exempt yourself from the power of genes that rule every moment of your existence from the very beginning to the last breath you are going to take. It is the defective nurture that kind of mutates the genes of smile into scowling genes. Smiling has been associated with survival; and so smile is natural to life.

TELE-SMILE

Any time you talk on telephone
Wear a pleasant facial expression
Your expression is transmitted
Quite accurately wirelessly or on wires

And if you smile while talking
Your smile is also sent out with your words
And your smile is detected by the listener
Very precisely and pleasantly
Above claims have been confirmed
Through true-life experimentation
A smile alters your verbalization

Of the words of the speaker
Same words uttered in anger love or sympathy
Go on different amplitudes and frequencies

Stand before a mirror
To watch and test your image
Frown and utter *I love you*
Smile and mumble *I don't love you*

To your amazement
Smiling and mumbling *I don't love you*
Will sound like if truth be told
I really love you

For your joy and peace
Let your smile be on your lips, eyes and in your tone
When you want or give
Love, favors, orders or simple service by a phone

Smiles overly faked and exercised may cause depression. Many professions mandate smiling faces to portray an impressive image of their corporations; flight attendants, call-center technicians, skilled secretaries and online sales persons are taught to wear smiling faces all through their conversations because such expressions are believed to walk through space waves to yield satisfactory results and sales. To such wage earners, end of the day is end of the daily smiling misery. One who has natural smiling disposition is most suited to the aforesaid professions.

Smile can run a life smoothly. No matter what neurologists have discovered or may discover, they shall never conclude that a sincerely smiling face is not hiding a happy intellect behind it. Just as clean, unassuming and plain clothes in the long run may induce clarity into a man's brainpower, agreeable facial expressions may stimulate neurons with tranquility.

What will you do with all the wealth you have amassed?" was the question asked of many highly compensated CEOs of large corporations. The response was: "We can only tell you what we would not do with it, and it is that our offsprings will inherit only a little of it lest unearned wealth is the poison that kills ambition". Historically, with rare exceptions, all outstanding inventions, great discoveries, and most rewarding business ideas came of the minds and muscles of men and women of ordinary means. So, a wealthy birth is a poor ground for ambition to survive, but poverty is a better ground, but not a sure bet, for an aspiration to smile and grow

Smile has one mode that hides in the mind and heart without any external appearance. Some name it inner smile; some call it silent peace of mind. Buddha is the symbol of this smile. This is the smile that has no fake component and is the best healer of all intellectual ailments. This is the smile that smiles only at the smiler. Inner smile is like a potent prayer to realize true serenity of the soul. A big mass of stinking garbage made of anxiety, hatred, jealousy, enmity and many sick feelings keeps on accumulating in most brains. Inner smile turns all that trash into tranquility.

SMILE OF THE *SELF*

An inquiry into an abstract but real phenomenon called consciousness is unique. It is the only impenetrably complex state of biological system that is being (and has to be) researched by itself. It is no wonder that biologists, philosophers, psychologists, and all other serious researchers who start writing about consciousness very soon shoot off some tangent and completely lose sight of the real subject. Thousands of books and papers have been published on consciousness, but only a little of all the information contained therein relates to the primary question – what is it they should be talking about?

What makes consciousness - the true reality of the 'Self'- the ultimate mystery? The subject and the object for this introspection is one and the same entity. Can we really conceptualize the essence of I, Me, You, He…? Can we ever understand who IT is that thinks, remembers, computes, smells, walks, eats, digests, dies, kills, and gets killed? These questions are not easy to grasp. All distinguished philosophers have written some sense but a lot of seriously articulated gibberish about it. All messengers of God - prophets – descended to the planet earth and told their followers- the men - how God bestowed them with souls that no other living beings have, and how their souls shall be examined after they die. All religious leaders have somehow invented or discovered that man has an ingredient in his person that cannot die or be killed, that in a certain way he is immortal. The concept of soul and its substitutes can be found throughout the documented history and is fundamental to all present day religious faiths; without such a super-natural ingredient, we cannot claim to be superior to the rest of the life forms and that will be a tragic blow to our ego.

Smile germinates at conception; this fact has been confirmed. Then right after birth how it escalates depends upon how it is nurtured. An infant's brain sucks without any discrimination all that goes around its sensory mechanisms - seeing, hearing, smelling, touching and tasting. This sucking action does not operate upon only on a smiling environment but on all good, bad and neutral settings. Destinies are thus founded or obliterated into the young minds for all their long lives.

Smile counters evil nature of man; this is one gesture that makes man look good. The best component of all cultures is wearing a peaceful smile. Due to whatever and various reasons, the majority of population of humans for most of the documented history have not been fortunate enough to laugh and smile. Daily chores just to procure food and shelter have been too overwhelming for men to relax and not plan for the next day, next year and next decade.

Very large part of the world population has always been too busy in gluttony and greed to laugh and smile.

CAN A POLITICIAN CARRY A SMILE!

Most humans are basically morons. They want a ruler to rule them, to run their legs, livers, and lungs, to provide them with a livelihood, and to give them food and shelter. With their mass-power these morons want to attack the very segment of the society that creates the means of their livelihood.

The rulers empowered by the mass-power of the shackled morons also despise the most productive and ingenious minds of the society. These rulers scream and shout that they are working hard for their morons, whilst doing their best to stifle any real progress that can be made by geniuses.

The morons have invented the word 'charisma' to run after. Female morons want a male charismatic face to be ruled by; male morons don't have much of a choice, they have to accept one of their own kind. Happily, human morons smile by the smiles of their master politico. Having born free, all die in the chains of their charismatic rulers.

Mark Twain was a genius to recognize and declare that the truest class of criminals is the class of politicians-in-power. This is the class that rises up from the lowest stratum of a society and ends up ruling both morons and all the productive people. Once a politician captures power, he does not relinquish it until he dies, becomes pathologically senile or is disgraced by one of his many criminal acts. The government of the people, by the people and for the people is essentially government of the tiniest brains, by the craftiest hearts and for the laziest bodies. The major aim of any government is to kill, control and curb freedom of the populace.

Be it the worst or the best, on the face of a ruler by any nomenclature, a smile, if any, shall be absent or fake.

SMILE OF DEATH

Don't forget!
I gave you life
Only for a while
For reasons, I don't reveal

Alas!
You don't understand
I'm always around
Around plants and trees,
Tigers, peacocks and bees,
Kings, emperors and queens,
I treat all, rich and poor,
With equal tender loving care

Without me,
Life would be a rotting entity,
It is due to my omnipotence,
New life comes into existence

I take you,
Sometimes surprisingly,
Other times amazingly,
Mostly, very slowly and painfully

Live, as long as I let you,
With love, wisdom and humility,
Don't ever hurt your honey,
Fancy, but with sincere modesty,
Work for fun, not just for money,
This is the only way to be cheery

Don't hide in a hood,
And forget about any should or could,
I shall take you,
Whether you are wicked or good,
Of all life, I'm the end of the end,

So, I'm the one,
The only one,
With perpetual smile,
I give life, I take life,
So smile, keep smiling,
For I close on sooner on
Those who live out frowning

The learned philosopher was a professor at a university of high repute. He loved solitude, and had the unshakable belief that the idea of being married was dim-witted. How could one squander so precious a life in perpetuation of human- brand! Man didn't have the right to be born repeatedly and endlessly; he was, in every possible way inferior to any life form other than his own; so did our philosopher muse.

The philosopher loved to take a leisurely walk every morning and evening to watch the splendor of sunrise and sunset. He thought and spoke of the mysterious God, Nature, Mind and Soul. People listened to him in awe; he could explain any mystery to anyone very confidently.

Inside his mind, the philosopher missed a loving companionship; he felt alone and lonely. People greeted him wherever he went, but no one saw a friend in him.

One element of his experience confused him. Why did that old couple living in a little hut on his daily walkway appeared so content with life? One day he stopped at the hut and saluted the old man, and asked him if he was happy. The man responded that he had nothing to be unhappy about, and he was not sure if there was any wall between happiness and unhappiness. The philosopher was dumbstruck at the profound philosophy of this man. The philosopher found, this man was ignorant, illiterate and poor but truly wise and judicious.

On top of the list of life's priorities at any time is to have a body that functions without mental or physical pain and affliction. Despite abundance of knowledge on how not to abuse our bodies, we do an excellent job of treating them with superbly mutilated and adulterated nutrition and a terrible mixture of emotions. We have a little better control on what we put in our mouths than what we put into our heads. What goes into our heads determines our health, happiness, and future significantly more than anything else. We can make our heart and head fountains of smiles, whether we are rich or poor. Unfortunately, 'progress' has successfully blocked our minds from enjoying the scenery of nature that all keeps on changing. Most of us are so locked in four walls, or are always in the shadow of huge buildings, that even the serenity of sunrise or sunset is now strange and unfamiliar to most of us.

What is knowledge!
What is ignorance!
The answer seems simple,
But truly, is impossible

Look back, a thousand years,
Our ancestors had less doubts,
About their beliefs,
Than we have today about ours

Once there were only five elements,
Earth, sky, fire air and oceans
And man was content for millenniums
We peered deeply and were helpless
How deep is the depth of any element!
The answer is agonizingly impotent.

Start splitting a particle,
There is no way to ascertain,
When splitting is possible
And when impossible

As knowledge gets bigger
Faith in the knowledge shrinks faster

We are vastly ignorant,
Of what we are ignorant
Knowledge and ignorance,
Have no walls in between

Too sure of your knowledge,
Too sad of your ignorance,
Either way you are bamboozled,
You shall never know,
What you don't know.

How wise is a wise man!
How scholarly a scholar!
The answer varies, as time goes by.
So, follow the best strategy,
Keep on smiling, as years roll by

HOW SIMPLE!

It is fruitful to believe that no achievement is impossible if we set our minds to it; this belief produced great inventions, inspired many discoverers, paved roads for many successful followers, and it did let us land on the moon, explore the heavens, and reach the innermost heart of the atom. Perfecting our lives with good emotions and pleasant smiling gestures should not be hard if we try just a little harder

It is in praise of the Mysterious Unknown Almighty, that a prayer keeps the wandering mind in reins to enjoy inner smile of the soul. No reason is good enough to rationalize or irrationalize this eternal reality. All non-believers are doomed since the only recourse they have is to booze-up their brains to rot their bodies and suffer from deadly boredom.

Smile can be award-winning or award-losing. This category has been invented or discovered by an orthodontist. You don't have to be a great politician, scientist, lawyer or movie-star to wear an award-winning smile. You have to simply comprehend the subtlety of your facial features, color and shape of your teeth and jaws, your hair style, and so on. Then just surrender to the skills of an orthodontist, and you shall be on your way to win a smile that shall win anyone you want to.

Smile has a spiritual link with the mind. Spirituality has millions of explanations and billions of followers; not much can be agreed or disagreed upon in the matters of spiritual philosophy; it rests strongly on the foundation of faith, and has been unshakable despite all the tremors that came and went in the history of faiths. Spiritual faiths create spiritual smiles that keep minds and hearts peaceful and tranquil. Don't look for reasons because faith and reason don't mix.

Smile has been categorized by one inspired casino researcher into a magic variety of '10' kinds to empower the decimal system. These smiles relate to gambling environment. (1) Master smile – All dealers wear it. It is dull, dumb and precisely deadly. (2) Down-the-drain smile. It is the smile that should be expected by any intelligent gambler after losing big time. (3) Gloomy smile - It sits on a gambler's lips all the time. (4) Confused smile – of a blackjack player who has no idea what he is into. (5) Good night smile – I'm tired, see you in the morning. (6) Waitress-Waiter-Smile – smile for big tips (7) Surprise win smile – because a win is always a statistical surprise. (8) Old senior smile – worn by gambling seniors. (9) Rich loser smile (10) Get lost smile - smile from a gorgeous female toward hopeful males for hopelessness.

SMILE! YOU'RE HERE

Before God sent you to the planet earth
She did not tell you what you must do after birth
Your arrival was celebrated with sweets
By mom, dad, friends, uncles and aunts
Do you wonder!
Why you are here!

Parents taught you to walk, talk and play
And instructed never to wander away
For many years you were schooled
Without being taught how not to be fooled
Do you wonder!
Why you are here!

All education was about making money
Not how to make life a wise journey
That is why, most of your long years
You suffered from jealousy and fears
Do you wonder!
Why you are here!

Mother prayed, you should live long
Friends advised, you should be strong
Priest taught not to forget dear God
Father told, you should be moneyed
Do you wonder!
Why you are here!

Family wanted, you should love and care
Boss ordered, you should work harder
Kids wished, you should take them places
So they can explore God's mysterious spaces
Do you wonder!
Why you are here!

All your life you try honestly to please many
Working hard for years very sincerely
Sometimes you fail, sometimes succeed
Sometimes laugh and sometimes cry
Do you wonder!
Why you are here!

Remember, God sent you here
To do some good for sure
So, laugh and smile as long as you are here
This hurts few and pleases lot more
That is why you should not wonder
Why you are here!

Time to depart is always near
For, to God you are very dear
That is why do not wonder
Why you are here!

Our minds have a zillion times more to discover than what has already been discovered. It is very inspiring, a great challenge, and a limitless opportunity to smile about. The inquisitive minds should love to smash into more of the wonders of Mother Nature. Nature of humans is a complexity that is more complex than all other wonders

A SMILE
Petite
or
Prominent
is
Eye-catching
In a
Micro-moment

**HAPPINESS
IS ABOUT CHOOSING**
Preservation over Devastation
Innovation over Imitation
Humility over Pride
Generosity over Greed
Love over Hatred
Serenity over Ferocity
Amity over Enmity
Compassion over Cruelty
Liberty over Slavery
Vigor over Lethargy
Tranquility over Hurly-burly
Knowledge over Ignorance
Courage over Cowardice
And
Most Importantly
**SMILING
OVER
FROWNING**

SMILING LOVE

Love is the emotion that relaxes our mind, brings peace to our whole being and fills our surroundings with all kinds of joy. It also improves our health, strengthens our immune system, and in sickness makes us feel less sick. Loving and being loved is far more important than any other worldly or physical achievement or possession. Unquestionably, those who are deeply, truly, selflessly and with full sincerity in reciprocating loving relationships, are the most fortunate people on the surface of the earth.

Love softens our speech. It makes us respect our fellow beings. It rewards us with cooperation from others. It increases our work efficiency. It makes any difficult task easy to handle. It runs our lives with most pleasant perfumed lubricant. It makes us kind, gentle and compassionate. Love is the only food that nourishes our minds and bodies without depositing any fat in our arteries. Love is the only music that can be played without any instruments. Love is the only speech that can be heard without ears.

Here we are talking of 'love' that lacks any sensual tinge; and of 'love' that demands or expects nothing in return, but in reality naturally reciprocates a deep concern for the welfare and happiness of all parties in this loving relationship. In its purest and most natural form this love exhibits itself between parents and their very young. In its next natural form it becomes such a bonding force between two persons that not only they can not live without each other but they would be ready to die for each other.

True love does not require any rules and exhibitions to be felt and exist. A smile is all that is needed to propagate it.

Soul's Sweetest Secret

Smile

Smile blurs much of divergence between a chubby body and perfect petite attractive figure. A smiling chubby and flabby personage overshadows everyone in any big festivity. People spontaneously want to hook up into happiness. An association with a shattering pretty face has a life that does not last long in a string-less culture that espouses freedom very freely at all costs. Chubbiness carries with it an innate attribute, and that is prettiness of big smiling cheeks.

TAKE IT EASY
DON'T BE SPEEDY

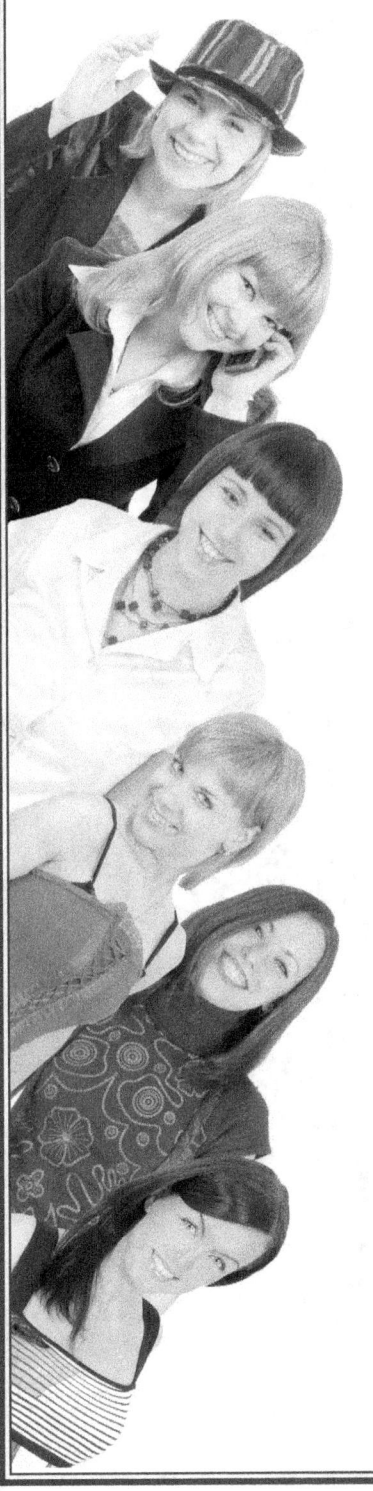

Smile to slow down not only the rat race but all races of life. Technological evolution takes our physical body from here to there too fast; it also takes our emotions from top to bottom or bottom to top too swiftly. Imagine, if all our wishes were fulfilled instantly, if the food we ordered was on the table in a moment, if we could create a masterpiece in a week, if we could learn any skill in a month or two; most terribly, if a newborn became an adult in two years. Life under all these conditions shall be monotonous. Let the life move unhurriedly, if you want to enjoy it SMILINGLY.

SMILE SUMMARIZED

Finest Lipstick, Real Thing, Best Companion
Universal Hello, Dazzling Ornament, Heart Seizer
Free and Precious, Secret of Real Beauty
Fresh and Ready, Charming Personality
Soul of Life, Chain for Unity, Power-Tool
Freedom Festival, Birth Reward
Stress Relieving Remedy

CELEBRATE IT!

SMILE
With
Optimism
For the road ahead
is
Beautiful, Inspiring
Promising and Exiting
Is the future a black tunnel
of desperation or a bright road
of hopefulness! It is all in the
mind of the perceiver, how it is
observed.

MAN Vs VEGETATION

In the realm of plant-life, the life that sustains all human and animal life, every tiny seed yields thousands of edible fruits and seeds of its own kind, and thereafter each one of these new seeds yields next batch of thousand of seeds. This geometric progression goes to infinity and shall never end; and when this ends, all life shall end.

One noble lesson man can learn from a fruit-laden tree is that its branches bow in humility, with a kind of smile, when it is ready to bestow its produce without any obligation. In contrast, man of fruitful-fortune turns into an upright haughtiness.

Man in the perpetuation of his seed has only perpetuated chaos in the realm of plant-life, the life that is vital to the perpetuation of his own seed. The claim that he makes of his brain-power is shocking.

How do we greet or should greet all whom we meet or encounter in our social, family and business life? A pleasant facial expression and some kind of physical closeness has been a part of greetings at all times, in all nations and cultures. A pleasant facial expression has been the common denominator, this expression is nothing but a soft and sincere smile of eyes and lips. Physical closeness has manifested in many forms. Strong hugging, kissing, touching feet or hands, sitting very close, shaking hands have been some of these manners. Greeting with folded hands is unique to Hindu-culture. It confirms lack of any assault. Hands are held close to the heart to show respect from the most vital organ of life. Bowing of head and a soft smile always accompanies folded hands. In some religions, prayers are offered with folded hands.